Awaken your ...

VISIONARY MIND POWER

~ BOOK ONE ~

THINKING Beyond
Habitual THINKING

By Integrating Mind Tools of:
HYPNOSIS, MEDITATION, MINDFULNESS
& POWER OF ATTRACTION

BRUCE J FRANCISCO, CH, NLP

1st Printing May 2018

2nd Printing July 2018

Published by Francisco Production Co, LLC

PO Box 270, Westbrook CT 06498

ISBN 978-0-9627372-2-0

1. Self help techniques 2. Psychology

Cover Photography by Kelly Francisco

Photo of author in front of his plane.

"As a kid, I always heard the statement
that man only uses 5% of his brain potential …
I'd to scratch my head thinking …
Why don't we use it all?
What if I could use 10%?
That would be twice as much as most people use!
What if I used 100%?
What would that be like?
How does one get there?"

Think of this book as an
owner's manual for your mind
that you were never given.

Study this book intensely and carefully.
As then, you may find the answers that
you have been seeking all your life.

CONTENTS

Part II

MEDITATION

Part III

HYPNOSIS

Part IV

VISIONARY MIND POWER

Integrating MEDITATON, MINDFULNESS, SELF-HYPNOSIS
& POWER OF ATTRACTION into your life.

To my wife Kelly

ACKNOWLEDGMENTS

Thank you to all those people who helped me gain the insights to put this book together. Special thanks to Cyril and Mikhail who helped with the initial drafts, and to Mark and Becky for reading through the final drafts. All the feedback sent to me have pushed me to refine the process of expressing the profound principals that would be best received.

My wife Kelly has been most helpful. She was always there to help read through the drafts and point out elements of confusion. Her objective criticism during the writing of this book helped me be clear in expressing the concepts expressed, so as to best understood by most readers. Her love, patience and support, as well as her constructive criticism, will always be appreciated.

I am grateful to the authors who have influenced me along the way from Carlos Castaneda, Wayne Dyer, Roy Masters, Deepak Chopra, and Eckhart Tolle only to mention a few of the several hundred books read over the years including parts of the Bible, as I reflected on my own ongoing search for, "who I am and what am I suppose to do," as I tried to make sense of my own life.

Thank you to all the people who through seminars, shows and even in private who I have shared these principles that gave me the opportunity to develop my ability to express my thoughts and ideas. These interactions helped me develop insight into other viewpoints so I could learn to convey these ideas in a way that most could relate.

Thank you to all the trials that life offered me allowing me to find higher ground within the crazy confrontations of life. Like steel that is forged and made stronger through excessive pounding, these trials taught me lessons that evolved into wisdom that helped refine my approach to life itself. May these insights also inspire others within their situations in life.

I often say that no matter who you are and whatever you're doing within the perceived problems you may have, that beyond all the possible circumstances you find yourself, we don't know who we are and why we're here. We have a natural instinct for survival, but beyond that, the purpose of life seems to elude us. The best we can do is seek to find what Love is, and seek for a better understanding of who we are. From there, we can hope to find our purpose and ultimately learn to use our Visionary Mind Power to manifest amazing life experiences. Again. It all seems to come back to a quest for a better understanding of God and Love, then finding the guidance to act upon life's unlimited opportunities to express and share who you are, and inspire those around you.

Part I

INTRODUCTION TO MIND

*The only thing in this world
worth possessing
is peace of mind.*

Chapter 1

INSPIRATION
FOR THIS BOOK

Ever since I was a young boy, it intrigued me when I heard a commonly heard and spoken statement that man typically uses only 5% of his brain potential. This always bothered me which raised questions I often pondered: "Why don't we use it all?" "How can we at least access 10% or more?" "How can I control the thoughts that travel through my mind?" We have always wanted to control our minds, but no-one has ever shown us how.

Since my early college days, I have had a profound curious interest in understanding the mind. One of my first courses in college pertained to "mass media" and how easily influenced the population was by various media sources. My studies also led me to an interest in hypnosis and an understanding of how easy it was to fall under the influence of suggestion from an outside source.

It became apparent that if one is hypnotized, one may not fully realize how influenced their mind is from outside suggestion. This was when I began to realize that I may not have full command of myself and that I wanted to learn how to take greater control of my mind and 'perceptions of my reality'. Ultimately, my search was to understand how I ended up on the path I did get on and how to get back on the path that God intended me to be on – the path that had the most heart.

Learning to meditate was what began to teach me to take control of my internal thoughts and not to be subject to all of the world's influences and pressures. The techniques I learned, nearly 38 years ago, not only calmed my mind but helped me to not give into the unwanted thoughts that were likely going to cause me pain and confusion (doubt and fear).

As my insight into mind control became extensive, the realization of my mission became more apparent; to help educate others on mind control techniques in order for them to be able to overcome unwanted habits, self-induced doubt, depression, phobias, and especially avoid the influence of the subtle unconscious manipulations from others. I also wanted to learn how to guide people to their intuitive foundational understanding of how their mind works.

My goal was to devise a system that would help people realize how to strengthen their minds and develop insight on how to manifest greatness in their lives with a simple understanding of how the mind works. With the right guidance and understanding the use of simple mind tools, one can achieve greatness they never thought was possible yet was always available and right in front of one's eyes waiting to be discovered.

Albert Einstein once said that the mind, although it has amazing capacities to acquire knowledge, he proclaimed:

"Imagination is more important than knowledge.
For knowledge is limited to all we now know and understand,
while imagination embraces the entire world, and all
there ever will be to know and understand."

We all have access to this infinite creative intelligence. So rather than only using 5% of our mental capacity, perhaps we are 95% asleep and have the potential to awaken and tap into this unlimited creative intelligence within our subconscious by learning a few straightforward techniques of the mind.

We, humans, are extremely hypnotizable suggestible creatures of habit and function from the subconscious whether we realize it or not. Our subconscious is influenced easily due to our reactions to our world experiences and often distracts us from our true intelligence and manifesting potential.

Meditation and mindfulness help one to understand how to become objective towards the thought process, while hypnosis powerfully influences and affects the underlying process of the subconscious mind and ultimately what we attract into our lives. All hypnosis is self-hypnosis, therefore understanding how to influence our subconscious the way we choose, would be an ultimate accomplishment in maximizing use of one's mental capabilities to effortlessly and consistently move towards personal goals with minimum effort.

Aside from writing books and creating self-help CD's, I developed a motivational, fun and inspiring hypnosis show. The show was not to make fun of the participants as some stage hypnotists might portray, but to have fun with the volunteers along with the underlying intent to inspire the crowd and the participants. In time, my shows evolved to become a customized keynote presentation tailored to any theme that migrated into a hypnosis demonstration. The hypnosis demonstration powerfully revealed tools of the mind and made known the concepts of Visionary Mind Power (VMP) that anyone with a mind can use. Meditation, self-hypnosis, mindfulness and power of attraction are always the foundational principals.

While demonstrating the power of the mind and how easy it is to be hypnotized, audiences can witness the potential of the mind first hand. The volunteers on stage experience directly the potential of the mind and the power of tapping into their subconscious (creative intelligent imagination) and leave the stage with positive, powerful suggestions along with a heightened state of awareness, a higher level of confidence and greater self-esteem.

Whatever your intent may be, understanding how to use these powerful tools of the mind synergistically can help anyone lead a happier and more prosperous life and avoid getting trapped within the negative rabbit holes of the mind.

Note: In the context of this book you'll hear me use the term rabbit holes. At one point we were going to make the title of this book, "Escaping the Rabbit Hole." But we decided that "Thinking Beyond Habitual Thinking" was more appropriate for the material you'll about to read.

Nonetheless, think of "rabbit holes" as the mental traps that life presents to many of us day to day. Ultimately, the insights from this reading will help anyone to not fall in too deep and quickly avoid or hop out before getting too lost.

Chapter 2

WHY IT'S IMPORTANT TO READ THE OWNERS MANUAL FOR YOUR MIND

If we only had access to a manual
for the mind to read in the first place!

I am a pilot and have been flying for over 45 years. My flying lessons and schooling started when I was 14 years old. Suppose I took you up for your first flight in my Cessna 172, and then, suppose you were thrilled to experience the freedom of flight. You were enthralled so much that you decided to learn to fly and work towards getting your private pilot license.

Your first thought might be to hop onto a plane and take lessons with a flight instructor. As a mentor that wants you to be a safe pilot, I would tell you to take a lesson or two in the plane, but more importantly, go to ground school, buy the textbooks and prepare yourself to pass the FAA written exam for your private pilot certificate.

After passing your FAA exam, then take the lessons in the plane. Now with greater insight from your accomplishment, your lessons will be more educational. Your learning curve and questions will be more intelligent. You'll better know what you're doing and why you're doing it. Ultimately, you'll be a more informed and safer pilot. When any pilot earns his pilot certificate, he soon realizes he just got his license to learn. When the learning process ends, (or so you think), the danger and safety risks go up.

In the same way, you could explore your mind and its immense potential. It's not like we ever had an instructions manual for the mind, but if we did, what could we have learned that would make our life easier, less stressful, more prosperous and full of joy?

Every year I confront thousands of people and help many to appreciate the value of understanding the tools needed to increase the ability of the mind to reach its highest capacity. For years we provided a meditation CD and self-hypnosis CDs. It was noticed that people would use the CDs with no basic understanding of what they're doing and why they were doing it. As a result, their progress was minimized and just abandoned. It became apparent that the people whom I was able to spend time with to explain the process experienced greater results and continued their learning experience (seekers of understanding).

Think of this book as an owner's manual for the mind to reveal a starting point for your basic understanding of the mind. As with a private pilot's certificate, it will be your vital foundational information as you develop your lifetime license to learn.

If you already meditate, the material covered will enrich the insights you already have and help you gain greater benefits to your practice.

Perhaps just this book will be an inspiration to set you on your path, but as I learned a long time ago, my search is never-ending. Welcome and thank you for joining me on this powerful journey.

Chapter 3

THE PATH TO MINDFULNESS

*"When we get too caught up in the busyness of the world,
we lose connection with one another – and ourselves."*

~ Jack Kornfield

This book is the first of a three book series (Visionary Mind Power
– VMP) that will reveal to anyone how you can reduce stress
by becoming more mindful of your life experiences and achieve
goals with remarkable ease. It will also act as your guide to
greater personal and professional satisfaction – more than you
ever thought possible.

In Book One, we will discuss Meditation, Hypnosis, Mindfulness
and the Power of Attraction, all under the main parts of the book
Meditation and Hypnosis. We'll discuss and reveal what they
are, how they work and how they can be used synergistically
to unleash your greatest potential and help anyone to avoid the
deceptive rabbit holes within the mind.

Note: Over the years the concept of "Mindfulness" has emerged.
When I discuss "meditation", think of mindfulness as the state that

meditation will bring you to as you walk through your experiences in life.

There is a razor's edge difference between meditation and hypnosis. By enriching your insight into these processes of the mind, you will be able to recognize the distinctions necessary to use these powerful tools to command your mind more effectively, and therefore, integrate mindfulness into your life.

My personal experiences and struggles in life have caused me to search for answers. I always wanted to take control of my thoughts but never knew how. Among the many inspiring encounters along my pathway of life experiences, approximately 38 years ago, my journey crossed with an American family in California who had spent many years in India. This family had different free-spirited energy not common to me at the time.

They took me in and made me feel like I was a part of their family. The mother and I often chatted endlessly about things about life's meaning, and for years after I had moved onwards, she magically would call me whenever there were times of uncertainty in my life. The father was a hypnotherapist to help people overcome bad habits and life problems. He also ran a small spiritual seeking group that spoke of basic truths that resonated well with me at the time. The father and I often spoke much about things that were meaningful and deep and about life's purpose. He introduced me to various techniques of meditation and insights that helped me develop a deeper understanding of myself.

Years after, I lost touch with them, but the impact they had on me set me on a path that changed my life forever. I always knew one day I would write a book to help others who had the same desire to understand the mind beyond the typical mindset. This book will help you acquire the control of your mind that you have always wanted. Haven't you always wanted to take control of your thoughts, but no one ever showed you the "how to?"

What unfolds in the following pages will reveal principles, wisdom and techniques which have helped change the lives of thousands. You hold in your hands a guide that will help you tap into the power of your mind, control your destiny, and enrich your life and the lives of others.

I remember two great movies from years ago that I will recommend to you. One is "What the Bleep Do You K(now)", and the other is called "The Secret." Many have asked me if I have seen these movies. My reply was "great movies, but The Secret is no secret." It was a wonderful collaboration and marketing effort. However, the movies do not teach one how to control one's thoughts. The movie suggests what can happen when you do control your thoughts and what consequences occur if you cannot. There are no specific techniques taught to harness the extensive powers of the mind.

The methods needed to accomplish meditation and hypnosis and therefore mastering mindfulness, are not time consuming or expensive. They only require a small investment of your time and the willingness to experience their usefulness, nothing more. You have to be willing to use a little energy to tap into this abundant energy supply. Your mind is like a muscle; the more you exercise with techniques that work for you, the more strength you will discover within. The stronger your mind becomes, the more potential of your mind will unfold.

If you decide to follow this path, your life may never be the same. It will be my honor to help you find your own path. You may have looked almost a lifetime for the answers on the outside that were always within. Like with the old saying, "you can bring a horse to water, but you cannot make him drink," I encourage you to discover the techniques that work for you and to utilize them to develop and increase your ability to utilize your Visionary Mind Power within your journey of life. I am here to answer any questions and encourage you to continue your search for the enlightenment you seek.

Chapter 4

THE MIND

"There are no constraints on the human mind,
no walls around the human spirit, no barriers to our
progress except those we ourselves erect."

~ Ronald Reagan

What is more fascinating than the mind? We all have one. We function every day and night within its realm, yet we scarcely understand how to use our mind to its highest potential. Let's face it; the human mind is the greatest, most powerful, and mysterious gift we'll ever know. Human beings have shaped societies and developed fantastic creations and innovations that have evolved the world as we know it – simply with the mind.

As mentioned, we never had an instruction manual to learn the secrets an owner's manual could reveal, but if you did, how would it make your life better? We went forth in life figuring things out the best we could and then adapted. You might have thought that all is good, but perhaps you've always known in your heart that there must be another way to carry on but didn't know where to find the answer – or even ask the question.

Most of us have worked with software on our computer or apps on our smartphone for a time, thinking we have mastered all its functionality. Then, someone (perhaps 1/3rd your age!) shows you a little trick that was right there in front of you, and you might exclaim, "No way, that's amazing – that makes total sense and makes things so much easier."

Well, you're about to witness that within the pages to follow. If you read carefully and perhaps re-read this book, you'll learn to understand how to use the power of your mind to focus on exactly what "you" want for yourself. The goal here is to learn some simple mind tools that will enhance everything you do. There is a meditation technique that goes along with this book – you might have a CD that came with this book, if not, you can listen directly or download free at:

www.RelaxationMeditionCD.com

It is highly recommended that you practice the meditation technique daily as this will enhance your understanding of the material to follow and more effectively help you integrate these powerful principals into your life's journey. Think if you were learning to fly. It would make sense to learn about what the controls do first, then take a lesson to practice and fully learn the material in practice.

Get ready to explore the amazing power of your mind and how a greater understanding of hypnosis and meditation can offer you powerful tools to reduce stress, become a master of mindfulness and also motivate positive change for you and the loved ones in your life.

Part II

MEDITATION

*"Meditation is not a way of making your mind quiet.
It's a way of entering into the quiet that's already there."*

~ Deepak Chopra

As a certified hypnotherapist and a teacher of meditation and spirituality, I found that the first thing one needs to do is learn to control their thoughts. A person's inability to reach a trance state and benefit from the power of self-hypnosis seems to arise from their inability to quiet and still a restless mind. Mastering and understanding meditation and hypnosis together empowers one to control their thoughts and change any behavior.

Once you learn to master your thoughts, which meditation will help you gain insight how this is possible, you will better able to become more mindful as you go through your life experiences. From here, you can begin to see how to use the techniques of self-hypnosis to influence your subconscious and command your life path that has the most heart, successfully.

We'll begin by exploring meditation and learn what it means to become aware (the mindful watcher) of one's thoughts, thereby making the mind (thought) control a possibility (keeping desirable thoughts and dismissing not so desirable ones and recognizing the difference). We may then begin to utilize the power of self-hypnosis in the best way possible, which then allows powerful positive changes within the subconscious without a struggle.

Note: One last thought: as you progress into the chapters to follow. Although we have two main parts to this book – Meditation and Hypnosis – understand each part will discuss and reference meditation and hypnosis to each other throughout the book. As you begin to read through the treatment of meditation, the term hypnosis will be brought up prior to our full discussion on hypnosis to help you understand the distinctions between these two mind tools. Just bear with this as the concepts will become clearer as you progress.

Chapter 5

WHAT IS MEDITATION?

*"Prayer is you speaking
to God. Meditation is allowing
the spirit to speak to you."*

~ Deepak Chopra

Meditation is a conscious purposeful, disciplinary action, where the practitioner attempts to "leave" the ordinary "conscious mind" to achieve a profound level of relaxation or awareness. Meditation has been used for thousands of years. Its use was generally for spiritual practices. Many types of religions encourage meditation and prayer to bring one to a state of spiritual enlightenment. Meditation can enable anyone to improve concentration and increase self-awareness.

Jesus said, "Be **still** and **know**..." (Psalm 46:10).

If we can learn to use the meditation exercise to help us strengthen – **still** – our minds and have split second recognition of a thought that is not useful, we would then see a choice of perception that we previously had not considered – **know**. Keep the good thoughts, recognize the difference, and learn how to walk through our experiences, rather than our experiences walking through us. Have you ever had your virus software on your computer quickly stop a suspicious threat to help you determine if it were safe or not? This is a possibility this book attempts to reveal that we may have never considered until someone like Jesus showed us the way – in our mind.

The thoughts in our mind often have an unconscious or hypnotic effect on our awareness and tend to mold our internal perception of reality. Perceived reality can often have little to do with true reality. How many times have you worried only to later find that this created anxiety, was a waste of time and energy, and had nothing to do with the final outcome? We tend to torture ourselves with fears of failure, doubt, judgment, worry or the cheap opinions of others which often distort our view of true reality.

Meditation is a tool that cuts through these illusions (deceptive rabbit holes) of the mind, revealing the true reality of a situation to the practitioner. It guides one through a maze of confusing thoughts and perceptions, bringing forth realization of a new fresh path of the mind which may ultimately lead one to greater happiness with the ability to manifest anything into your life. Mastering this capability opens the door to using what we call our Visionary Mind Power (VMP).

Meditation is also a way to release one from mental prison, and will help reveal inner truths that have been hidden for so long – under the surface of the conscious mind – within the subconscious. If most people were asked to stop thinking, they would find it difficult as they would try to stop thinking using thoughts. Meditation is a way to receive a revelation of the mind through the mind without the use of thought.

Chapter 6

MEDITATION — ACTIVATING THE GATEKEEPER

The benefits of
meditation are like having
anti-virus software for the mind.

Meditation is the sword that helps anyone
cut through the mind's illusions.

There is one concept you will find, repeated throughout this book and that is; we all have the freedom to choose the thoughts that imprint our minds. Many people have wanted to know how to take control of their mind, but have never known the secret to mastering their personal ability to control their thoughts and perceptions. The mind is like a muscle. We nourish and exercise our bodies, but largely ignore the muscle of our mind's potential.

If we don't learn to master our minds, random misleading and/

or dangerous thoughts can overwhelm us and cause us to attract undesirable circumstances. When we react wrongly to an experience or allow our minds to become full of self induced doubt and gloom, we risk internalizing within our mind, erroneous interpretations of our life which may then become our reality – in our perception. We tend to attract what we think about all day long, as in time, we may find these perceptions begin to show up in our reality – power of attraction.

By learning to be in command of our thoughts and understanding what it means to become "aware," we are able to maintain a view of life's big picture and not distract ourselves into the traps (rabbit holes) within the menial occurrences of day to day life.

Meditation can become a sword that helps strengthen our ability to pierce through deception and confusion. It helps us learn to quiet the mind's chatter and have the option to recognize and dismiss false truths. By training one's mind to remain calm in stressful situations, we can learn to remain objective when interacting with the world's pressure.

Would it not be wonderful to have total control of the thoughts that appear in our mind? Ideally keep the good stuff and dismiss the bad? If our reality is made up of the thoughts and perceptions that travel through our mind, then learning how to choose the thoughts that we allow to stay foremost in our minds would give us the ability to change our life, or at the very least, the way we look at it!

I read a book several years ago "Long Pilgrimage, The Life Teaching of Shivapuri Baba," by John G. Bennet. This man, Shivapuri, lived to age 137. At age 18, he went into the forest of India and came out at age 35. During this time he lived among tigers and wild animals in harmony with the natural environment. He then decided to walk from India to England to meet the Queen. After meeting the Queen, he walked back to India, and at age 85 lived again in the forest, teaching spirituality until his death. On the cover of the book, there is a photo of Shivapuri at age 112 – he looked no older than 50.

Among his last words before he died were, "keep a barbed wire fence around your mind and only let in that which is good." He then said, "Live right life, worship God," then he got up from his bed and asked for a drink of water, sat down and said, "I'm gone," he laid down and passed away. He truly lived an extraordinary life.

It is our reaction to our experiences that we internalize in various ways that often confuse and confound us. Think of a leaf in the wind with no control of its destiny, it is fully subjected to being pulled in countless directions, representing the characteristic of a weak mind.

Wouldn't it make sense to use your Visionary Mind Power to draw a mental picture in your mind of exactly what you want for yourself? Using your VMP is to learn to stay focused on your "perfect principal" as you see yourself becoming like a rock that is unmoved by confusing world influences. The untrained – weak mind – risks being influenced by anything and everything that it is exposed to.

More than ever the smart phone revolution has added greatly to this world of distraction we live in. A study just prior to 2015 by a researcher at the San Diego Supercomputer Center (SDSC) at the University of California says, that by 2015, the sum of media asked for and delivered to consumers on mobile devices and to their homes would take more than 15 hours a day to see or hear.

It's quite common anywhere in public situations these days to see people glued to their phones, not talking to each other while eating at restaurants and walking together down the streets. I often see people working out at the gym, strolling their babies alongside the streets and dangerously driving among many other situations as they are engrossed on their smart phones. No one is paying attention as they are focused solely on the screen of their phone – hypnotized!

TO LIVE IN THE WORLD BUT NOT BE OF IT

Today, among other things, it seems like there is a strong fight for where your attention is on various "media screens." Nothing is wrong with using all these devices, but it would be important if you can learn to not be distracted and keep focused on your vision, in the picture in your mind, of the perfect world that you would want for yourself. Keeping your attention on your purpose in the midst of life's distractions (rabbit holes) is paramount to having your ideals and goals – manifest.

A well trained strong and informed mind actively utilizes its awareness (strength) as a filter to the world; a barrier to its deceptive and negative influencing potential. If you think of your mind as being like a computer that is always exposed to the internet – world pressures, stresses and influences, then meditation is a technique that activates and enhances your built in anti-virus software of the mind. We shall discuss more on this concept in the subsequent pages of this book. But for now, understanding the process of meditation can actively protect the computer of your mind from malware and malicious viruses that are consistently trying to invade your subconscious in your day to day life.

Not only should one learn how to meditate, but one should be aware of how and why the process works. By mastering our Visionary Mind Power, we can stay more mindful within the instances where our attention is distracted from our life goals and ideals.

Note: Think of "ideals" as being the foundational principals of perfection that you want to see within yourself. Taking the time to establish your ideal will help you develop a foundational principal as a base point for all you do.

An example of an ideal can be to want to be a better listener. When you not only "think and speak about yourself" when communicating, you become more compassionate within your life relationships. With that "ideal" in place, you'll then find yourself listening more before you speak or prompting people in general to talk about themselves, so as to establish more effective communication. This "ideal" is more than likely to extend into all your relationships in your personal life as well as business.

Chapter 7

A SIMPLE MEDITATION TECHNIQUE

"Everything is created twice,
first in the mind and then in reality."

~ Robin S. Sharma

After writing this book, one of my editors asked me, "Hey Bruce, I want to know now... early into the book ..., how to meditate." So I've decided to put a simple technique here and there throughout this book – starting now.

Note: I want you to read this book with an objective state of mind. To read and follow these pages with points of reflection will enhance your understanding of your mind and the essence of the material. My goal for you is to experience this book from a clear state of mind. So when you come upon these reflection points...

Read through them slowly...

Taking on each suggesting concept ... like tasting an elegant dessert...

Gently and slowly scan the words that are enlarged in the font that follows...

Try to hear the silence between each word you read ...

For now ... let's take a moment to be in the moment.

Where ever you are, slowly read these words and let them flow in and out of your mind.

For a moment ... in this moment ... notice the sounds in the room you're in.

Listen ... keep listening ... every time you notice your mind is wandering ... stop to notice this ... and then re-engage in noticing all the sounds in the room you're in.

You'll begin to notice sounds that you were not aware of before... keep listening ... keep noticing all the sounds ... see if you can hear the silence.

It might seem like you just awakened to the moment. As if you were asleep in your mind and now you find yourself in the room.

Be here ... listen ... notice when your mind is not in the room – noticing the sounds – while slowly reading these words ... now ... re-listen again.

Thoughts might surface ... notice the thoughts ... don't engage into them ... notice them while noticing the sounds in the room where ever you are ... while your mind scans these words.

As you notice various thoughts that might arise ...

notice you don't have to be involved with the thoughts

as much ... as you are still aware of the sounds in the room.

The detachment from your thoughts gives you the option to let them pass as you remember to stay in the room.

Notice and distinguish two realities. One in the room (hearing the sounds and the silence)... and one in your thoughts.

You cannot hear the sounds in the room and be aware of the silence and be in your thoughts at the same time.

Now close your eyes and do this for a few moments before reading on ...

This is a simple meditation technique. For some, this may be all you ever need to know to allow you to pierce through your mind's illusionary

fixations and become more mindful where ever you are.

Most importantly, *keep it simple ...*

If you don't have our basic Meditation CD already, you can also listen directly for free if you go to:

RelaxationMeditationCD.com

But for now, just read along.

Chapter 8

FACTS ABOUT MEDITATION AND REDUCING STRESS

*"I've been using it for almost
40 years now – and I think it's a great
tool for anyone to have, to be able to
utilize as a tool for stress. Stress, of course,
comes with almost every business."*

~ Clint Eastwood

Over the years, clinical studies have confirmed the benefits of meditation. Many have had great success in reducing migraines, insomnia, irritable bowel syndrome, premenstrual syndromes (PMS), anxiety and panic attacks, as well as lowering levels of stress hormones, blood pressure and improving energy.

More than ever, doctors are encouraging meditation for the therapeutic benefits, and they are recommending exercises and mind relaxation techniques to their patients to help them remedy stress induced illnesses.

In her book, "Mind Over Medicine," Lisa Rankin MD clearly reveals, with scientific proof, how the body's natural state is healing when it's in the rest state. When the body is stressed and in the flight or fight mode (in which stress activates), the body releases cortisol that protects the body to navigate through whatever obstacle presently occurring. But the problem is, so many rarely leave this defense state that stress creates, and as a result the body doesn't have it's time to rest and heal, and therefore, the gate is open to various diseases that show up and take over. When the cats are away (stressed away from your true healing energy) the mice play (dis-ease).

Knowing how to minimize or stop our negative emotional reactions to outside pressure (stress) is a main characteristic of a strong mind. The truth is that life will always have what we perceive as problems that create stress. If we can subconsciously use our Visionary Mind Power to shift our view of problems as simple stepping stones to reach any desired condition, then we can shift the way we look at these experiences as lessons to overcome any obstacle.

Note here that: *"Emotion" tends to increase the ability of our reactions to our experiences to delude us.* We'll get into that in more detail as we progress.

Chapter 9

CHANGE CHOICES AND STRESS

Follow the paths that have heart ...

Ever since we are born to this life, we face a never ending journey of change to physical death. Life is change; based on our past encounters with life, we either perceive change as unpleasant or pleasant. To this point in your life you've had many changes that may have caused you pain or pleasure that caused you to change the way you look at things. These changes guided you to make new choices that ultimately helped you find a new path of life choices that served you well. The positive or negative emotion connected with these experiences may have influenced the good or bad choices you made going forward.

Visionary Mind Power – Book Two – "The Power of Pain" will deal with this principle more directly. Nonetheless, the essence of the principle is that, we have an inbuilt system of guidance in our physical bodies that saves us from harm. If you touch a stove, you feel pain that causes you to remove your hand quickly so your body doesn't destroy itself.

In the same way, if we can learn to subconsciously recognize that the pain we feel in our mind is trying to guide us, we more likely will learn to, and understand, that these painful feelings are signals to lead us to change the way we look at the situations we find ourselves. We then, can learn to follow our gut feeling in making important decisions.

Following your heart – The wise choices you make in life often lead you to higher ground, that lead you yet to making more wise choices that lead "ideally" to a less stressful and more harmonious life.

Following your pain – Haven't you always known that the situation you were dealing with was simply the way it was? Perhaps a part of you didn't want to face the truth and therefore you ended up making decisions based on what you hoped for rather than the truth. From here you end up making poor choices that lead you to making more unwise choices leading to more pain and discord.

Learning how to implement discretion over your thoughts in demanding situations will help you to stay objective – mindfulness. Staying mindful will allow you to make wiser decisions based on the truth of your situation rather than responding to emotional charged reactions that could lead to choices that are less desirable that would possibly lead to more stress and disharmony.

Ideally, you want to make decisions that create inner peace and happiness as you walk through your path of life. Meditation is an exercise that allows anyone to develop a strong mind that will be more objective to choose wisely as you confront the decisions you make day to day.

Chapter 10

WHO CAN BENEFIT FROM MEDITATION?

Anyone and everyone.

Especially nowadays with the stress of everyday life, meditation is for everyone. At one time it was a practice used only by mystics, yogis and philosophers for spiritual and religious practices. The value of the benefits of meditation is now recognized by many from all walks of life – from celebrities, housewives, business executives, doctors and other medical professionals.

I have performed in hundreds of schools around the country with my motivational assembly and hypnosis show which allowed me to get a feel of several types of school systems and programs. Meditation is a foundational principal revealed to the students during my presentations of hypnosis. Along the way, there has been more mention from students and teachers from schools that we perform who speak of learning meditation and mindfulness in class.

In order to meditate one does not have to be religious, nor must they dedicate their lives to the practice. We brush our teeth every day to maintain our dental hygiene. We don't think about it and it makes sense, so we just do it.

We clean our computer's memory with system tools that de-fragment the hard drive and use system tools to remove unwanted information which allows our computer to run more efficiently. Does it not make sense to clean the blackboard of our mind to rid ourselves of unwanted thoughts and meaningless information that clog our perceptions and our ability to focus on the truth of our reality?

Visualize yourself as having the immense energy of the sun. Yet the rays of light are scattered off into countless directions. If all the energy of the sun were to be focused in one direction, collectively directed to one area, an unbelievable laser beam effect would occur with the concentration of that energy.

So it is with our minds; meditation is a practice that empowers us not to disperse our energy in countless directions. Once relaxed and contained, we are able to focus our attention directly in any area of our lives that we choose with great intensity.

By becoming objective to our "thinking process," we begin to rise above frivolous and unimportant thoughts and thereby pierce through the distracting illusions of worry, doubt and fear. Additionally, meditation will allow you to cut through unconscious influences that often confuse you, increasing your self-confidence to keep focused on whatever you want and ultimately help you get back on the path that you were meant to travel.

Thought to ponder: Typically we don't think of animals that get stressed out with the need to meditate to become more centered. Animals stay centered more naturally – especially a cat. Think of a cat, sitting there purring completely mindful and in harmony with the moment. Yet within a split second with a laser beam focus it will pounce on an un-expecting target. Some would call this living in the "now", some who can call it living with mindfulness. Cats are amazing warriors that practice mindfulness instinctively.

Chapter 11

CUTTING THROUGH ILLUSIONS

with the sword of meditation ...

"Be still, and know that I am God . ."

~ Psalm 46

"Be Still ..."

Taking the time to exercise our mind to be in the moment gives us the ability to become conscious (aware – mindful). This process allows us to fine-tune our mind and enables us to view life from a clear and powerful objective state. Within this view, life's meaning often becomes clear, focused and logical.

As a child, brushing your teeth and washing up seemed to be an effort and a meaningless waste of time imposed on you by your parents. Yet as an adult, grooming and taking care of yourself is a habit that allows you to feel that certain integrity with maintaining yourself. So it is with training your mind to be still.

"And you will know the truth, and the truth will set you free ..."

~ John 8:32

"... and you will know the truth ..."

In the early years of my meditation practice, I was in such a rush. It was difficult to take the time to sit still. I would struggle to quiet and slow down my turbulent mind. For a period, I remember there was much pain associated with sitting still. What was the pain? It wasn't physical. The mental anguish was nothing more than giving up on thoughts that caused me pain, yet I felt I needed to hold on to them. Maybe I was just seeing the truth of my life that was always there, but never wanted to face. Perhaps I was holding onto the painful thoughts and perceptions for some sort of twisted security?. The mind plays tricks on each of us in different ways.

"... and let the truth ..."

When I began to sit still and learn how to quiet my mind, nothing particularly exciting seemed to happen. It was like waking up to the moment, where I could hear the sounds, smell the air and feel the presence of life. As I learned to hold my attention in the moment in life (mindfulness), things started to surface: my self-image, selfish intent, and the intent of others. The key here is to not judge what you see and simply see it for what it is. If you judge it, you quickly would fall away from the moment and lose your mindfulness.

Principal: The battle is best won, not battling.

As my interest in hypnosis grew, I also began to see hypnotic influences everywhere, from cultural influences, media influences to our day to day interactions with people. Life itself has a pattern of negative or positive (hypnotic) influence on everyone.

When people learn that I am a hypnotist, I'm often asked: "Can you help me stop smoking?" or "Can you help me stop eating too much?" Sometimes, they ask, "Can you hypnotize my wife?"

When you become adept at discerning and controlling your thinking process, one can use hypnosis to re-program your subconscious mind into <u>knowing</u> that you were <u>never</u> a smoker, nor had a <u>problem</u> with eating, but only <u>think</u> that you did. Knowing the <u>truth</u> that you were never truly a smoker, nor had an eating problem will allow you to be free to recondition your mind to <u>know</u> that you <u>are a non-smoker</u> and re-program your eating habits to <u>know</u> you <u>don't have an eating disorder</u> and are now <u>attracted to eat</u> what your body <u>needs </u>to be healthy."

"...set you free ..."

My rational response is always the same. Let us first start with the idea that you are already hypnotized into thinking that you can't stop smoking or overeating. Once you begin to understand the nature of your perceived problem, we can use the power of meditation to de-hypnotize you.

As far as hypnotizing your wife or husband is concerned, I would recommend the art of listening to your spouse and allowing yourself to really know where he or she is coming from, and from there, let them know that you know and understand their point of view. Getting on the same page is paramount to ultimate communication. As mentioned before, *If you're not a part of the solution, often you're a part of the problem.*

When one begins to understand the intricacies of the mind, you will find that there are no problems that cannot be resolved in human relationships.

Chapter 12

BREAKING THROUGH THE DIFFICULTY OF MEDITATION

(sitting still)

*"All problems with man stem from
his inability to sit quietly in a room."*

~ Blaise Pascal

We say that we can relax, yet our mind wanders uncontrollably. The purpose of meditation is to allow the mind to become calm, alert and focused.

Some believe there is only one way to meditate, yet there are many paths of meditation. The purpose should be the same; to bring one to an objective state of mind. When in this state of mind we are clear, transparent and unbiased.

There are many ways to meditate. Mostly, the common denominator is to begin with a process of relaxation by focusing your attention on a single thing (thought, sound, object, etc.) until your awareness of a timeless, peaceful consciousness emerges, while the chatter of your mind's thoughts fades away. Every time you notice your attention shifting to a thought rather than the object of focus, gently but firmly bring your attention back to the point of focus.

Simply put, the "meditation exercise" will strengthen your ability to become conscious of your thinking process and ultimately allow you to rise above the influence of confusing thoughts and perceptions. Alongside your dream state of everyday life, you will have trained your mind to be aware of a safe place that will always be available in a split second. A mind that is calm and objective helps anyone to have more control in just about any situation – mindfulness.

RUNNERS' HIGH – A FORM OF MEDITATION

I am a runner, and when I do, I notice that in the beginning of the run, my mind is in a dream state. I don't think of it this way, but after several minutes of running, my mind shifts. The concentration becomes more focused on the trail and my body as it adjusts to the running state, and in an instant, there is a shift to a mindful state that feels as if I just woke up from an unconscious trance state. All thoughts and concerns that dominated my mind fall away and my mind becomes clear. It's kind of like the feeling of waking up from a dream.

This runners high that runners speak of is the shift to an objective state that meditation will bring one to. So in this sense, running can and is a form of meditation. My goal in this book is to reveal a deep understanding of meditation, so this "mindfulness state" can be brought forth in an instant whenever one chooses within any situation that they find themselves. Hence, using your Visionary Mind Power.

WHY MEDITATION IS INTERGRADED INTO
A STAGE HYPNOSIS DEMONSTRATION

Our standard motivational stage hypnosis show is often just a fun, entertaining event, but still, my style as a stage hypnotist is always to have an emphasis on the power of the mind. My goal is to have fun, but always leave the audience with a better sense of the latent possibilities of the mind. Within my pre-talk before asking for volunteers to join me on stage, I give the audience a sample meditation exercise to leave them with a takeaway to help reduce stress.

More importantly, within my induction technique used on stage, meditation is indeed the foundation that is used to slow the mind down and help the participants to focus their attention. It's important to clear the pallet of the mind, so the essential communication necessary for the suggestion is maximized. The participants always feel the effects of a clear mind, sometimes for the first time in a long time.

In my early years as a stage hypnotist at a casino, a 68-year-old woman who participated in the show offered a video commentary documenting her perception of her experience. She said: "I came here tonight thinking that this was going to be a joke... who can get hypnotized..." She stated that she liked some of the principals of the mind discussed in my pre-talk and therefore decided to volunteer.

She went into a trance on stage and was amazing in her ability to reach a creative childlike freedom one can experience when in a trance. She didn't remember anything that she did on stage, but more importantly, she said that she had been suffering for over 20 years from a family incident that she chose not to disclose. Her revelation was, for the first time in 20 years, she mentioned within the experience on stage, she told of her experiencing a new place in her mind that she now discovered not known to her previously. She felt for the first time in many years; she was free.

Note again: The meditation is used as a core base to induce trance, and a clear objective state of mind is indeed the by-product of a hypnosis session.

At first, most people find that sitting still is very difficult since they've never attempted to quiet their mind. However, be confident that you will gain results with a little practice as you are developing a new habit. Even if you are only able to take a minute here and there to practice, you will find that eventually, the process will become second nature, like brushing your teeth or combing your hair. Sometimes you may spend more time to be more thorough, and other times, maybe quick and to the point. As long as the process is enjoyable as you progress you'll look forward to the opportunities to experience the perceptual freedom that meditation offers.

Let's take another moment to be in the moment.

Where ever you are, slowly read these words and let them flow in and out of your mind.

For a moment ... in this moment ... notice the sounds in the room you're in.

As you're slowly reading this ... listen ... keep listening ... every time you notice your mind is wandering ... stop to notice this ... and then re-engage in noticing all the sounds in the room you're in.

Now let one of your hands hang as freely

as possible by your side ... now notice your hand ... notice the blood flowing through your fingertips ... slowly, be aware of your hand ... feel the warmth ... notice your hand might start to tingle or feel the warmth of the blood flowing.

Notice yourself at this moment ... as if you were asleep in your mind and now you find yourself in the room hearing the sounds ... reading these words ... with a relaxed, quiet mind ... yet aware of the energy flowing in your hand.

Be here ... notice your hand ... the tingling ... notice when your mind is not in the room ... come back to being in the room ... notice your hand while you slowly read these words ... now ... be aware of your hand again.

Thoughts might surface ... notice the thoughts ... don't engage into them ... notice them while noticing the tingling in your hand ... and the sounds in the room where ever you are ... while your mind scans these words.

As you notice other thoughts that arise ... notice that you can't be aware of your hand and hear the sounds in the room and be in a thought at the same time ...

Notice you don't have to be involved with the thoughts as much as you are still aware of your hand which is now an anchor for your attention.

Your detachment from your thoughts gives you the option to let them pass as you remember to stay in the room as you are ... still ... and aware.

Now close your eyes and do this for a few moments before reading on ... Read these words over again from the top if you'd like ... read slow and savor the moment.

There are two realities that are in front of you at all times. The reality of the moment, **"in the room,"** with your hand tingling, and hearing the sounds, feeling the sensations of the moment **"and"** your perception of your reality based from your mind's perceptions when you're **"not in the room."** To be able to flash back and forth between these two realities at will, allows anyone to become a master of using the tools of their Visionary Mind Power to create a fantastic wonderful life experience.

Think about that for a moment.

Chapter 13

SEEING OBJECTIVELY

helps break down communication barriers.

Be still ...

From a quiet place in our mind, we are better able to understand the truth of any situation. Knowing this truth, from this perspective, one will be able to make better decisions about the way one perceives the world, and be free to make more conscious choices premised by their newly found objective view of reality.

... and know

We often interpret our reality through our inventory of knowledge and personal needs and interests. This is why many individuals may view the same circumstances in a countless number of different ways.

People can attend the same movie; one person falls asleep, another wants to walk out, and yet another may feel it's the best film they've ever seen. We often have our viewpoint of any situation based on our perception that is molded from our inventory of thoughts, experiences and personal needs.

Conflict often arises between people because one may only hear or see "their" side of a situation. One who is "aware" (mindful) may be more inclined to listen and hear what the other is saying during a conversation, rather than only hear what one is "thinking." Simply listening can break down most barriers to communication by arming you with an understanding of the others perspective.

As you become a master of your thoughts, and learn to switch to a mindful state in an instant, you're likely to catch yourself within a conversation more attentive listening rather than reacting (not hearing where the other person(s) are coming from before you have your chance to speak). If truly objective, you will be more inclined to notice when someone is caught up (anxious, depressed, defensive, etc.) and therefore see options for better communication.

The objectivity that meditation offers can help bring a group of people to common ground. When at least one person learns to become aware – mindful – in any situation, the mind's illusions that create misunderstanding are broken down and revealed. Then, the common ground of any situation is more likely to become apparent. The result can often be less conflict and a greater capacity of understanding each other's perspective and enable the discovery of solutions that benefit the whole.

An objective mind will allow you to sidestep the confusion and disarm any conflict well before any misunderstanding could escalate. Remember, it takes two people to create an argument (accident), but only one to stop it. If you are attentive to becoming aware, you will find yourself disarming potentially bad situations and attracting great relationships to your life.

Practice: In your next conversation with your child, boss, spouse or whomever you speak with, resist the temptation to talk initially and take the time to listen to them and become mindful. As you do this, you will naturally be able to see a new option of communicating you had never noticed before. The more you do this, the more you will be able notice when to kick in your mindful state in crucial interactions.

Chapter 14

TO MEDITATE

*"When your attention moves into the Now,
there is an alertness. It's as if you were waking up
from a dream, the dream of thought, the dream of past
and future. Such clarity, such simplicity. No room for
problem-making. Just this moment as it is."*

~ Eckhart Tolle

THE BASICS OF THE PROCESS AND BENEFITS

As mentioned earlier, there is no single right way to meditate. The purpose of the technique we emphasize is to strengthen the mind's ability to focus on one thing and to notice when the mind starts to wander. Simply being able to bring your attention back to the object of your focus is the key. Think of the process as a simple exercise for the mind. The process will increase your ability to command the thought process. Whatever you decide to focus on, keep it simple.

The mind is like a well filled with water, contaminated with the impurities of random thoughts that leach in from the surrounding ground undetected. Understanding *meditation* and *hypnosis* together, allows us to help cleanse the mind of impurities, filtering our thoughts and allowing us to step away from hazardous thoughts that bring dis-ease into our lives and yet allow in the thoughts that inspire and empower our creative expression of ourselves.

As a hypnotist, I've come to understand that the mind's imagination builds images that become real to us thereby causing us stress. During stage hypnosis, when a suggestion is given to the participants, it takes a few moments (or longer for some) for the images to build in the theater of their minds. When the image is allowed to grow and mature, this intense fixation becomes their reality, as they express what is experienced in their mind with various levels of animation.

So it is with life. We may have a reaction to an experience on the outside that breaks into our mind and manifests as a distorted illusion (rabbit hole) in our perception – i.e. worry, doubt, fear and envy, or any other illusionary emotional responses to a situation. The initial reaction could be simple and no big deal, but the reaction often gets distorted and then becomes an illusion that seems so real to us that we lose our sense of the truth in the situation that we find ourselves. We often suffer greatly with this development of self induced doubt, gloom or resentment.

When one learns how to meditate with the technique we teach, one ultimately learns the importance of developing the ability to have split second recognition of the mind's initial false misleading reaction, enabling us to keep an objective view of our reality. Sure we might step into a deceptive rabbit hole, but one learns to quickly hop out.

As we learn to walk through our life experiences with mindfulness, we naturally learn to choose our perception, and thereby meaning of the thoughts we want in our mind or choose to not allow in our mind.

The thoughts that occur on a regular basis mold our base view of our reality and eventually manifest in our lives – good or bad as the subconscious doesn't have discretion. This process of manifesting the thoughts "we want" to dominate in our mind also influences the subconscious mind at the same time especially when there is emotion attached along with repetition.

Note: I am mentioning the concept of hypnosis here, so you may better understand the power that meditation reveals. By programming (influencing) our subconscious mind to move towards the things we choose in our life, we are using what is called "self-hypnosis."

To understand and act upon the tools of Meditation, Hypnosis and Mindfulness to control your perceptions of reality at will, is an action of using your Visionary Mind Power to manifest what some call the Power of Attraction.

This might sound confusing, so let's quiet our minds again for a moment while reading this so that it might begin to make more sense. We'll go into hypnosis in greater detail later in the book.

Let's take another journey into the moment ... to be in the moment.

Wherever you are, slowly read these words and let them flow in and out of your mind ... notice the sounds in the room you're in.

Watch yourself watch, as if you were watching yourself quietly reading ... listening ... hearing the silence ... experiencing a mind that is free of thought ...

Listen. Keep listening ... every time you notice

your mind is wandering ... stop to notice this, and then re-engage in noticing all the sounds of the room you're in.

Notice sounds that you were not aware of before ... keep listening, keep noticing all the sounds ... hear the silence.

Now notice the thoughts ... notice that you can make a thought dissolve as you observe it from a quiet place.

Unwanted thoughts may surface, notice these thoughts, but do not engage into them ... notice them while you're noticing the sounds in the room wherever you are ... while your mind scans these words.

As you notice other thoughts that arise, notice that you don't have to be involved with these thoughts as much, as you are still aware of the sounds in the room.

Your detachment from these thoughts gives you the option to let them pass as you remember to stay in the room. Now close your eyes and do this for a few moments before reading on.

Remember this ... remember to be aware of whatever you find yourself doing as often as you can.

Chapter 15

BREAKING THROUGH A STUBBORN MIND

"In order to taste my cup of water you must first empty your cup. My friend, drop all your preconceived and fixed ideas and be neutral. Do you know why this cup is useful? Because it is empty."

~ Bruce Lee

ZEN TEACHING

I've often heard the story of the Zen master teaching his student Zen as he added more tea into a cup that is already full. The tea began to flow over. The student said, "Stop your cup is flowing over." The master said, "exactly, you are like this cup, you are full of ideas. You come and ask for teaching, but your cup is full. I cannot put anything in. Before I can teach you, you have to empty your cup." If your cup is already full, how can anything else enter? If your mind is the filled cup, and it thinks it knows everything, how can any more wisdom come?

Techniques of meditation were first taught to me from the father of the family I met in California in my early twenties and also from the father of a girlfriend in Arizona while living in Tucson in the early 80's. At first, my mind's stubbornness created the idea that I "knew it all," and there was nothing that I needed to know. But soon, the practice began to open my mind to an elevated understanding of my mind and life. As I look back, perhaps I was mesmerized by my perception of my life itself. I <u>thought</u> I <u>knew</u> who I was, but all I <u>knew</u> was what I <u>thought</u> I was.

When I first began to drive at the age of 16, I thought I was a good driver. I was involved in many accidents within the first few years of driving. Quite frankly, a lot of them occurred within the first few months!

At age sixteen I also became an airplane pilot. Fortunately, I haven't had any accidents to learn from to date (my present age is 59). When I soloed (piloted the plane alone without my instructor) a plane on my 16th birthday, my instructor got out of the plane and told me to fly a solo flight around the airport traffic pattern. The flight around the airport and landing was successful. I knew what to do, but I didn't have the insight that one acquires with experience.

My pilot's license and driver's license were licenses to learn from mistakes and gain wisdom only experience can teach. Through the years of flying, I ran into countless problems that taught me how to make better decisions.

There's an old pilot joke: "Definition of the propeller: The fan that keeps the pilot cool. When it stops, watch him sweat." I believe every pilot fears to lose his engine in flight. When my engine failed climbing through 3800 feet one beautiful sunny Saturday morning, I didn't sweat! I flew the plane as instructed in my training. By executing the proper procedures, I was able to glide and find a suitable landing spot. As extreme as it may sound, the process was a wonderful experience, as the outcome could have been worse. The insight of experience and preparation teaches powerfully.

Is life not full of these lessons? It is recognized that Thomas Edison failed 10,000 times as he attempted to find the solution to a light bulb. If Thomas Edison were asked about his failures, he would correct you in saying each failure was a powerful lesson about what didn't work.

Now, with the basic mind tools understood and practiced that help remind you to be more mindful, one can travel through experiences learning from certain wrong decisions and perceived problems more efficiently. Learning to become the master of your mind can help anyone transcend perceived troublesome situations in their life. In the same way, you need the experience to become a great pilot, ready for any complication, and you need to develop a strong mind to be prepared to take on any challenge that life will indeed throw at you.

I once met an elderly man who repairs furniture. He stated to me that he "hated when people complained about problems." He said, "This isn't a dress rehearsal! I fix furniture. I'm always fixing things. That's what I do; I solve problems."

Enlightenment may occur when one realizes that there are no wrong decisions or real problems, but simply powerful lessons that teach us how to make better choices in finding solutions to life's inevitable encounters with perceived difficulties.

If we keep ourselves open to the flow of information that lessons (perceived failure or wrong decisions) teach, we might begin to notice and recognize the answers we were always looking for. Sometimes being stuck on pride (thinking we know it all) blocks our ability to receive the simple feedback from situations to correct and make the changes necessary to achieve our ultimate happiness. When we train our mind to react objectively and therefore stay more mindful as we go through our experiences, one is better able to see all perceived problems as gifts to enrich their insight into life.

The process of knowing is best understood when a person realizes that they don't necessarily know all there is to know. When this is acknowledged, a new path of unlimited possibilities opens up in the mind.

Action: Be still. Empty your thoughts and preconceptions and allow the unlimited creative potential of your subconscious mind to flow into your life.

Chapter 16

SCIENCE VIEW
OF MEDITATION

*"I stopped explaining myself when I realized people
only understand from their level of perception."*

~ unknown – a saying I saw on a bulletin board

From a psychological and physiological perspective, meditation helps us restore a balance between the left and right sides of the brain.

The left side of the brain deals with thinking, speaking and writing. When we are busy in a thinking state of mind, we are in Beta.

The right side of the brain deals with intuition, imagination, and feeling. Listening to the birds or the waves of the ocean, the brain functions with lower electrical patterns in a state called Alpha. We pass through the Alpha state just before falling asleep or just before waking up. During sleep, the mind falls into Theta or Delta.

When we are awake, the mind generally is in a Beta state. Daily, we are in Alpha only about one hour during a typical day. Meditation improves the essence of our life by increasing the amount of time in Alpha. By spending more time in Alpha, we expose ourselves to a mindfulness perception that allows us to define the world with objective views; in "the Now" before our senses can interpret our experience based on our personal history.

False interpretations of our experience may lead to conclusions of unnecessary negative emotional responses; doubt, jealousy, and fear. Learning to practice mindfulness when necessary as you face day to day experiences will allow you to keep a refreshing outlook as you encounter life day to day.

Thought to ponder: Know deep inside, as you pass the perceived problems faced day-to-day, that the past doesn't have to determine the future. This knowing – **Faith** – enables us to keep a bright outlook and perhaps recognize the opportunities that can appear like magic right in front of our eyes, where – **Doubt** – might have blinded us from "seeing."

Chapter 17

NO TIME TO MEDITATE?

*The benefits can create more time
and help you sleep better too!*

One may say that they don't have the time to meditate. However, if you just allow yourself the time to sit still, you will discover that in effect you are meditating. You may discover an incredible phenomenon. You may find that you are becoming more efficient in organizing what you do with your time – in your mind. The result is that you will find yourself less distracted and more focused on whatever you do; in effect, you'll be creating more time for yourself.

The time spent meditating is for you. It is to be done entirely by yourself, for yourself. This time allows your mind to become more efficient, and you'll begin to control where your attention goes. As your mind becomes calm and you learn to settle the chatter of your thoughts, you will find that you will be more able to focus on exactly what you want for yourself.

But often we feel we don't have time to meditate. When we finally try to sit still, our mind is flooded with all the things you have to do, and something inside you tries to convince you that you don't have time and there are things you need to do instead.

A POWERFUL STRESS-REDUCING TECHNIQUE

A simple way to reduce day-to-day stress and reduce the load of thoughts passing through your mind that tend to dissuade you away from spending quality time for yourself is to write down a list of things that need to be done as you think of them. Get in the habit to keep a notepad with you (or use a note app on your phone) as you pass through your day, and as thoughts of what you need to do come to mind write them down as you think of them. Get in the habit of "doing this now" as if you don't, often they will be forgotten.

This will reduce the pressure of trying always to remember things needed to be done as you no longer need to remember them, at the moment, in your mind. This also has the effect of cleaning the slate of your mind which allows your mind to focus more efficiently on whatever you're doing – mindfulness. At the end of the day, organize your tasks and ideas, and then write a list of what you want to accomplish for the next day.

A SIMPLE TECHNIQUE TO HELP YOU SLEEP ...

This is a wonderful technique to use if you find yourself not sleeping at night. Often when we finally lie down in bed to go to sleep, our mind tends to be flooded with thoughts of things that we need to do. If it's written down, you can be confident that you don't need to think of anything because all is taken care of as you can fall asleep with peace of mind.

My wife often asks me, what I am doing tomorrow, or later in the day. I find that it was hard to remember everything because I had written it all down. It wasn't necessary to remember, nor did I need to – or want to – engage my mind with the long list of tasks I needed to do. My response typically is, "I'm not exactly sure, it's on my list."

When we have all these items that would be on our list floating in our head, dreading what we have to do, and concerning ourselves with remembering everything, we risk getting caught up and stressed. If it's written down, we don't need to engage in trying to remember everything. We are better able to focus on the moment, right now, wherever we are, whatever we're doing. And still, at the opportune time, the task will be done, making your conscious time more efficient to focus on moments of mindfulness.

WHAT IF MY LIST IS TOO LONG?

However, if your list seems too long, this could create stress and frustration too. Here are two strategies to make the process less stressful and more straightforward.

1. Pick two things that need to be done first and "Do It Now." How to choose which to pick? Perhaps the things of priority that have been on your list the longest! After accomplishing the two major things, you may decide to do some more of the less important tasks. Now that the important tasks you've been putting off are accomplished, you'll find it's easier and less stressful to continue accomplishing more tasks, feeling relieved and less bogged down, as you now feel the energy of being more efficient.

2. Simply go over your list the night before and decide what is most important. From there, number each item from most important to least important. This technique will take away the guesswork and keep you focused on accomplishing your tasks, one item at a time.

Thought to remember: Be here in the <u>Now</u>. When it's time to engage in the tasks on your list, you will be able to be <u>there</u>, at <u>that</u> moment, doing only <u>that</u> which needs to be done in <u>that</u> Now. Never underestimate the power of focus!

Chapter 18

THE MUSCLE
OF MEDITATION

*Building a strong mind to break free from
deceptive mind illusions (rabbit holes).*

We often think of exercise and fitness to invigorate and to slow
the aging process of your muscles and therefore body. There are
also great benefits for health, heart, energy, and soul. Did you
ever consider that your mind is the most significant muscle of them
all and could very well be the cornerstone of ultimate health and
wellness?

What would be a strong mind? A weak one? How would you
exercise your mind and what benefits would it give you? If we
see the mind as a muscle and learn how to exercise it, we will
discover strength we never knew possible. You will find the power
and understanding of how to walk through life rather than have
life walk through you. It's our reactions to life's pressure that hypnotize, overload and overstress our mind.

Measure of strength: When you learn how to control your thoughts (keep good positive thoughts and dismiss bad thoughts and being able to discern the difference with the objectivity the meditation we teach reveals) and your reactions to stress, by exercising your mind's ability to become "mindful" every time you notice you're "not aware," in effect, you are exercising your mind to become strong.

A weak mind is one that cannot control its thoughts and is subject to reacting to every thought passing the screen of your mind, like a leaf in the wind always subject to the variable directions. A strong mind is like a rock, unmoved by emotional reactions to stress and thus master of your moments – and destiny.

A weak mind (untrained) risks being influenced by anything and everything that it's exposed to. Not only should one learn how to meditate, but one should understand how and why the process works. A well trained strong and informed mind actively utilizes its awareness as a filter to the world; a barrier to its deceptive and destructive potential.

The plain truth is you may get so involved in what you're doing that you get caught up in your perceived problems and become hypnotized by them. When one reacts to situations while "caught up," we risk coding the experience into our subconscious mind in undesirable ways. The trained, objective, and strong mind, via the instant objectivity the meditation technique teaches, has the power to allow one to see that they can choose the way reality is perceived, and thereby the way the experience affects us within. This view will enable one to notice opportunities in situations that might otherwise have been misinterpreted or missed, resulting in confusion and unnecessary negative thought patterns.

This is the frustration that you feel which blinds you from an objective view (stuck in a rabbit hole). To understand that we are often hypnotized by our fixations to thought processes (perceived problems), which are self-induced from our reactions to various stimuli, it is paramount to training your mind to become free in these (hypnotic) situations with the exercise of meditation.

When we learn how to control our thoughts and our reactions to stress, we also learn that we can change the way we look at things in an instant. As renowned author and speaker, Dr. Wayne Dyer said, "When we change the way we look at things, the things we look at change."

Lesson: Focus on the solution, not the problem.

The meditation technique we teach aims to train the mind to notice when you begin to get "caught up," noticing that this is happening in a split second and then becoming instantly objective once again – mindful – in the moment where ever you are, whatever you are doing. This ability is indicative of a strong mind – a mind that can consistently distinguish the truth from false impressions that deceive the mind as one walks through their experiences of life.

Chapter 19

TAKING A STEP BACK
FROM PERCEIVED PROBLEMS

The experience of jumping into a plane,
taking off and climbing above the clouds on a dreary day,
to only find a beautiful sunny day above,
is a reminder that one can at anytime access
a new refreshed outlook in any situation
when one learns to transcend their thinking state.

Have you ever noticed a time in your life where a situation seems to be too complex and frustrating? Of course you have! Who hasn't experienced stress? However, when you walk away from a problem frustrated, and take a break (put your attention elsewhere), you may come back to find an angle or a simpler approach that you didn't see when you were caught up in the scenario prior to taking the break.

We've often heard the statement when considering a decision, "let me sleep on it." In context of our discussions, that would mean to literally step away from a confusing decision, to break the hypnotic bias influence (hypnotized by the problem) so objectivity will help us view the clearer choice.

So as you take time away from a stressful life, you'll find that when you re-engage, your view of the situation(s) will become easier to evaluate because of your clear viewpoint. As you master your Visionary Mind Power you will learn to rise above your perceived problems anytime to achieve an objective state that will help you gain a perspective that reveals clearer choices.

Thought to consider: Never underestimate the value of spending quality time alone in silence. Time alone is the most important thing any of us can do for ourselves. Not only will it help reset your mind and perspective, but will empower anyone to be more focused and productive. As if you were the sun scattering it's energy off in all directions (stressed out), taking time to collect your energy will enable you to focus your attention with laser-like intensity when you confront your life experiences – mindfulness.

Lesson to ponder: You can never fail if you don't give up. Once this is understood on a subconscious level, you will more likely look for the solutions in every problem.

Chapter 20

FIND YOUR
SACRED PLACE

*"Your sacred space is where you can
find yourself over and over again"*

~ Joseph Campbell

Try to find a place that is peaceful for you. You will find it easier
to relax when you bring yourself to your sacred place where you
know it's your time collect and renew yourself from within. Try
not to meditate in bed, as you will likely fall asleep, yet this is a
wonderful way to fall asleep and wake up too! Most importantly,
find a place where you will not be disturbed. When you establish
your sacred spot, you'll find that you'll know it's your time for you,
to be still and be renewed from within.

As your ability to concentrate and quiet your mind improves,
you will find yourself being able to meditate (becoming aware)
anywhere – in a bus, at a stop light or a line in a grocery store.
Eventually, life can become a meditation (mindfulness) experience.

You will learn to take the situations that once caused stress and uneasiness and now make them into an opportunity to become more aware.

This simple practice could very well be the missing link to the control of your mind, and therefore ultimate happiness, you have always wanted as you pass through your life experiences.

Chapter 21

ACTIVE MEDITATION – MINDFULNESS

We are creatures of habit.
Most of everything we do is habit and a
function of the subconscious mind – good or bad.
Meditation helps us see the difference.
Mindfulness allows us to live the difference.

Many of us spend our time sleepwalking – similar to being in a hypnotized state. We respond and act automatically (habit) within much of the things we do day to day and often are unaware of what is happening around us. We may be waiting in a line, on a bus, driving or working within the scope of routine repetitious actions that help us be more efficient. And yet, at the same time, we are often lost in our thoughts, playing out scenes from our past, pre-playing conversations or visualizing events to come – daydreaming – at the cost of losing precious moments in the present.

For example, how often are you driving down a road forgetting that you're driving, until you pull into your driveway? Only then, you realize you weren't paying attention, and you were in some sort of trance. You may have been listening to the radio or on your cell phone while driving and possibly forgetting where you are or where you're going.

You were lost in the theater of your mind – trance. You snap out of it when a policeman pulls you over or if a car pulls out in front of you and perhaps a near-miss occurs.

The real question is: Would you have been speeding, or come to a halt completely at the stop sign or had that same possible accident if you were living in the moment, and not lost in the hypnotic trance in your mind?

Waking up to the world – Mindfulness: As you walk through life each day, try to experience the sounds, scents, and colors fully. Experience life from the "present." Let nothing pass you by. By actively hearing, feeling, listening and sensing your surrounding environment, wherever you are, at the moment, you are actively meditating – practicing mindfulness. Learning to become conscious of the present in all situations allows your mind to wake up and become aware of the true reality of any given moment.

Practice walking: When you walk down a path that you're familiar with each day, try to become aware of yourself walking down that path. Try experiencing mindfulness as you walk. Notice the people, get into the awareness of what they are thinking and feeling. See and notice the details in the visuals in front of you – the colors and feel of the sunset or sunrise, the vibrant flowers, and the smell in the air or the movement of the leaves in a tree. The more you notice while you are consciously aware in the moment, the more intrigued you will be with all of life.

Practice driving: Be aware of where you are as you drive down the road. When becoming more perceptive – mindful – you will notice how driving takes on a new experience. Feel the car, notice the scenery. It takes two people to create an accident, and one to stop it. Strive to always be the one in control and aware of the moment.

Practice in conversation: You will find yourself to become a better listener. In your next conversation try to listen to what the other person is saying and what their point of view is. There are always two sides to every story. Most of the time you might be thinking of your next response, planning the next thing you'll say – missing and not truly hearing what the other person is saying. As we truly listen and feel where the other person is coming from, the better we can communicate effectively in all situations that we encounter. Once the other person feels that you understand them, the more likely they will be listening to your side of the conversation as well.

As we become better at observing and listening in our life, we should begin to notice things about others and ourselves. This awareness could be the beginning of a new dimension in our lives. A life that is being enriched with new information about our "present" moments, allowing us to make better decisions about what we say and do during the time we have each day.

Note: Active Meditation is practicing Mindfulness.

Chapter 22

UNDERSTANDING HOW TO USE MEDITATION ...

to release phobias or post traumatic stress.

Phobias and unpleasant experiences of the past can be overcome while in deep meditation. While sitting still in meditation, things of the past will surface in its own time. As the meditation allows you to become extremely objective to the moment, experiences occurring in the past can be coded differently as you re-experience the past event from an objective state, found in meditation, at the moment.

As an experience surfaces from the past viewed from the stillness of meditation, this becomes your opportunity to code the experience differently as you re-experience the past event by observing from a safe, solid foundation in your mind. This process of recoding the way we react to stimulus in therapy is called Neuro-Linguistic Programming (NLP) will be brought up in more detail in Part 3 of this book.

When we react to an occurrence, we risk re-awakening the experience into our minds based on our interpretation of the aroused emotion of our past encounter. We can never remove experience from our past, but we can recognize how we reacted and change the way we remember and re-code the experience – using Visionary Mind Power to think beyond your habitual thinking.

If we had an original negative reaction to past experience, we might have induced a traumatic emotion of fear or anger. Our memory – subconscious – recalls this experience in the present when some instigation reminds us of the past event. It could be simply a scent or a song playing or a particular time of the year. It could be depression induced by remembering a past holiday season, which in turn can trigger one to react to the new season negatively.

Many people that suffer depression during the holiday season remember a depressing feeling that is reminded when some stimulus triggers a negative memory experience. Past unpleasant emotions flood back into our minds and overcome us in the present.

An example of this is PTSS (Post Traumatic Stress Syndrome) experienced by many soldiers in combat. They often experience traumatic emotional experiences on the battlefield. After the experience, they engage back into life and don't remember the horrors they experienced in their conscious minds. A few months later, a year or 10 years, an experience (stimulus) on the outside sets off a vivid memory that haunts them in their present state. In varying degrees, PTSS affects many of us in many ways in the subtle everyday battlefield of life.

Lesson: The past does not equal the future.

An example would be: If when a child, you were always attempting to do simple tasks on your own, but, one of your parents scolded you and made you feel that you weren't capable of doing anything right. As you go through life, you might feel confident to take on a new challenge, yet find yourself always self-sabotaging opportunities for fear of success. Hence, the mental subconscious pain of remembering your parents reprimanding you and therefore emotional pain attached to success.

In meditation, you can re-experience these scolding's your parent had given you. But now, in an objective state, you can re-experience (re-code) this interaction differently. You can now say to yourself, and see, that maybe your mother or father only had a protective concern that you might hurt yourself as a child or they may not have known any better. Perhaps, they may have had an experience of pain growing up that they were trying to protect you from? They never had the intent for you to carry this difficult experience forth into your life.

You might leverage this in your mind, that their intent in scolding you, was that they only wanted you to be careful not to make the mistakes they made. Looking even deeper, you might see that your parent(s) may have had the same fear ingrained into them from their parents that they unconsciously passed onto you. In this sense, you might begin to see this simple truth and now realize a new way to look at this conditioned thinking process.

This truth can help you to forgive your mother or father for not knowing what they were doing to you, which in turn will help prevent you from passing this conditioning onto your children or others in your life. Now you may confidently begin to carefully move forward with a new perspective as you take the unlimited risks that life offers with unlimited reward potential.

If you can begin to understand a new way of looking at things, in your mind, you can change the way you perceive experience in amazing ways!

Chapter 23

MEDITATION IN SUMMARY

"The highest possible stage in moral culture is when we recognize that we ought to control our thoughts."

~ Charles Darwin

The purpose of this book is to create an understanding and provide – reveal – the powerful tools of the mind. As mentioned earlier, when we came into this world, we did not receive an instruction manual on how to use the mind to its greatest potential.

Meditation allows us to become objective to our thoughts and the experiences we encounter. Once objective, we can begin to focus and understand what it means to master the thought process of our mind and our interpretation of our experiences. We can begin to understand what it means to differentiate between possible viewpoints of the same situation, and perhaps even change the perceptions in our mind – Thinking Beyond Habitual Thinking.

Giving up unwanted thoughts may seem awkward at first. One

may think that worry is a normal thing. To let a worrisome thought process go, and replace it with a positive vision, is an amazing transformational process that has always been available to anyone willing to take the leap and begin to exercise the mind's ability to rewire the way it processes information.

We now will see, and learn to understand, that the thoughts we have in our mind determine the way we perceive the world we experience and the situations we attract to ourselves to (Law of Attraction). The subconscious mind doesn't care or know if positive or negative ideas and thoughts influence it. This part of our mind cannot tell the difference between reality and an imagined thought or image (we'll discuss this further in the next section, Part 3 on Hypnosis).

Meditation helps us see the difference.

Mindfulness allows us to live the difference.

Mastering Visionary Mind Power is learning to understand the secret of consciously monitoring and perhaps controlling the influence to the subconscious mind by staying more mindful in your situations you confront in life.

What we continuously think about will eventually manifest in our lives, simply because we're continually programming it into our subconscious – self-hypnosis. As it is with the habit of driving home and not thinking about it, which is a subconscious process taking no effort, one can now learn how to be moving towards whatever goal or vision consciously desired without any effort on their part – Visionary Mind Power

This concept can work for or against your true desires. If one were to continually think negative thoughts and worry about what they don't want to happen, one is using the Law of Attraction to work against themselves. It's kind of like negative goal setting. This thought process that people manifest might be attracting the same situation to themselves over and over; re-enforcing the very thing they don't want to happen. We will discuss the Power of Attraction in more detail in Part 3.

Now let us explore hypnosis in detail ...

Part III

HYPNOSIS

*"Our subconscious minds have no sense of humor,
play no jokes and cannot tell the difference between
reality and an imagined thought or image. What we continually
think about eventually will manifest in our lives."*

~ Robert Collier

Chapter 24

WHY IT IS IMPORTANT FOR ANYONE TO UNDERSTAND HYPNOSIS

*We don't think of it that way, but before we had any habits,
we were little children exploring the unlimited possibilities of life. We
gradually accumulated habits that eventually helped us define who
we are – ego. Habits allow us to function more efficiently as
we pursue our life experiences on earth.*

As mentioned in the last section, we are incredibly suggestible hypnotizable creatures. We never thought of it that way, yet whether we realize it or not, taking on suggestion good or bad is very much a part of our everyday life. The process of hypnosis in therapy or self-hypnosis is a process of re-hypnotizing our subconscious for more desirable tendencies and habits.

We all are creatures of habit. The habits we have are mostly a learned function of the subconscious. We mainly function routinely from our subconscious. Before we had any habits, we were just little children experimenting with life gradually acquiring habits that eventually helped us define who we are in this world.

If you can see this as all true, one might then be able to see how to put this truth – knowledge – to some good use. Let us learn to recognize and keep the good habits and change the bad ones or the habits that might not be useful anymore.

Habits are good as they make our life more efficient. Or, habits can be bad as we unconsciously habitually do things that might be harmful to ourselves or others.

Habits are sometimes formed in our past that served us well then, but simply are not useful anymore and need to be changed. Often we don't even notice the bad habits that we develop that control us, as habitual behavior is hard to see in oneself. When we finally realize we have developed a bad habit, it might be too late, as now, a process of thinking, saying or doing anything has become a subconscious process. In time, someone that truly cares about us points out that we have a bad habit, or we might then realize we have an undesirable tendency and therefore begin to seek a way to change to a new habit.

As a stage hypnotist, many people often feel some level of fear when they consider the idea that they might become subject to hypnosis. This fear is based on their perception that they would "lose control." My goal here is to reveal that most of us are hypnotized much of the time in our everyday life nonetheless, by the routine things we do day to day – good or bad. To me, it's more daunting to realize that we don't have as much control as we think concerning how we are influenced. By understanding the process of hypnosis and meditation, one can learn to disarm many influences that are not desirable by learning to live our lives with mindfulness.

In the subsequent chapters, we'll be discussing various ways to look at and understand hypnosis. We'll repeat the same context in different ways so you can begin to get the big picture and scope of how your mind works. It is my goal to deepen your knowledge of Visionary Mind Power, so you can recognize the conditions and subtle actions of the mind to act upon, that make the most sense to you in your perspective. Ultimately my goal is for you to gain greater insight into the subconscious processes of your brain, as you learn to awaken your Visionary Mind Power.

Chapter 25

WHAT IS HYPNOSIS? THE PROCESS

*"The mind is powerful, and you have
more control than you think."*

~ Scott D. Lewis

(Self) Hypnosis refers to the stimulation of a heightened state of awareness of one's psyche; where the mind is held in a constant state of indivisible concentration, allowing better communication between the conscious and subconscious mind. Hypnosis can, therefore, help a person view a past situation with a more rational mindset; objectively and impartially allowing the subconscious brain to accept and implement a certain behavior that reminds the conscious mind of what it needs to know or do.

A hypnosis session opens a channel through which the subconscious can directly receive suggestions, which allows the possibility for the effective removal of mind-blocks and mental obstacles. The suggestions received affirms the need for a change of a mental behavior such as fear, anxiety, negative emotions or unwanted habits. This, in turn, will lead to a positive change in demeanor.

Many people are used to hypnosis being portrayed in movies and on television as a situation where a hypnotist who has special powers instructs a person, under his command, who cannot resist from obeying him as if under a spell. This is a misleading representation of the actual state of hypnosis.

Hypnosis is a natural state of mind that everyone, myself included experiences every single day. Hypnosis is suggestion that is accepted. A characteristic of hypnosis is that you don't know or care that it's happening.

Have you ever found yourself engaged by a project that focused all of your attention on the task at hand and time seemed to fly by? Have you ever tried to speak with someone who was so engrossed in a movie, project or a phone conversation that you had trouble getting his or her attention? Have you ever eaten a bag of potato chips and found yourself scrambling for the last chip at the bottom of the bag and reflect that you don't even remember opening the bag? Or remembered lighting the cigarette as you snuff out the butt? Or forgetting that you poured yourself a drink as you slurp the last sip?

Trance is a natural state of mind that most of us experience daily. Mindfulness is to experience all that we do unconsciously – consciously. As mentioned in the last section, the muscle of meditation allows for a stronger mind, a mind that can become conscious – mindful – at will, in almost any situation, hence using your Visionary Mind Power.

THE CLASSIC DRIVING EXAMPLE OF A TRANCE STATE

Each day, we fluctuate between the conscious and subconscious states of mind – a process achieved by adaptation. Each state of mind helps control the "mechanics" within the activities contained within our life. Indeed the process of functioning from our subconscious mind makes our life more efficient. We tend to multi-task all day long as we naturally move between the conscious and the subconscious.

Perhaps you were relaxing as you drove home from work, returning from the post office or to the gas station, then as if in an instant, you pull into the driveway and exclaim to yourself, "How did I get here!?" During that drive, your subconscious mind is aware of everything that is happening, but consciously you're thinking about things you need to do, thinking of things you might do at work, things you wished you would have said or done in a past interaction or engaging into music, etc.

Do you recall the details of that drive? I doubt it. Most people do not consciously drive their vehicles. You don't say to yourself, "I must put the vehicle in gear, release the parking brake, check over my shoulder for oncoming traffic, signal to turn left, then turn the steering wheel to the right and now drive the vehicle straight and stay in this lane." That is hypnosis!

The power of your subconscious mind did all the work as you were immersed in a relaxed trance state known as hypnosis. Your subconscious mind was working without any conscious effort, ultimately leading you to your goal (home) unconsciously – habitual actions at work. All the while, your conscious mind was focused elsewhere.

Understanding hypnosis and how to use self-hypnosis will create the possibility in our mind for this process to benefit us in almost any area of our lives. So without any effort on our part, we can always be naturally moving towards what we want, rather than led amiss via unconscious manipulations from other people, our spouse, our children, our co-workers, suggestive media, etc.

WHEN CAN WE ACCESS A PERFECT
TIME FOR SELF-HYPNOSIS?

How about the time before you go to sleep? Or in the morning when you slowly wake up while you lay in bed so relaxed and aware that it's time to wake up, but are so relaxed that you don't want to move. You might still hear the sounds of everyday life going on in your house or wherever you are, but you are so relaxed and rather stay in the dream (hypnosis).

This is a natural state of hypnosis. This is a wonderful time to learn to become aware of your thoughts, change them if necessary and build your visions of exactly what you want to manifest into your life and or your day. This is an example of self-hypnosis and also what successful people do to keep themselves focused on their goals in life.

COMMON HYPNOTIC APPLICATIONS

Many have used hypnotic influence and successfully modified behaviors such as:

1. motivation
2. confidence
3. attitude
4. focus
5. goal orientation
6. stress levels
7. weight
8. smoking habit

Beyond the list above, any specific behavior change is possible with the use of hypnosis.

Most people try to make behavioral changes based on self-discipline and willpower. The problem with this is that it is an inefficient and ineffective way to facilitate long-term change. Hypnosis is much more effective for behavioral change in affecting the individual on a subconscious level.

THE BATTLE IS BEST WON BY NOT STRUGGLING.

The real power of hypnosis is the bypassing any need for willpower, by making a change at your foundation level within your subconscious mind. By working with your subconscious, we bypass the conscious mind's arguments and therefore what takes hold in the subconscious mind simply becomes a new habit.

I recently overheard a conversation of two girls about to start a diet program to lose weight. The girls going into the program were excited to "try to lose weight." They were telling a couple of overweight girls about this program. The overweight girls told them, "sure, you might lose weight while doing the program, but once you're done with the program, the weight is going to come right back!"

This mindset is so true! Which is why all those special diets don't work, because the change is simply not a subconscious change, it's a simple fix that focuses on the problem – trying to lose weight – but doesn't solve the basic habit of eating on a subconscious level.

If your mission/vision is to see yourself as a slender person who integrates exercise and healthy food with smaller portions, hypnosis will allow you to take these suggestions into your subconscious mind and make them a reality in your perception. The more one can use their Visionary Mind Power to stir up emotion along with the new pictured image of themselves, the greater the chance the suggestion will take hold into the subconscious. Advertisers spend billions on ads charged with emotion to be more effective in getting messages into the minds of their target audience. This is your chance to do this for yourself. More on this within chapters to follow.

It is the equivalent of loading a software program on a computer; once it's in place, nothing can change it until new programming is loaded or that program is erased or upgraded. You simply will be programmed not to have the same behavior, and you do not need to make any sacrifices or struggle. You will see yourself being healthy, slender and exercising as a part of your everyday routine to maintain the new vision of yourself.

By working with your subconscious, we bypass the conscious minds arguments and therefore what takes hold in the subconscious mind becomes a habit. Your conscious mind will then automatically adopt the subconscious behaviors to achieve your goal. It happens automatically, similar to driving your car home, or to any familiar place, while your mind is focused on other tasks and thoughts.

STARVING FOR UNDERSTANDING

Within the stage hypnosis shows and keynote talks that we perform all around the country, I am in an interesting position to get direct feedback from many types of people within various social and cultural situations.

Sometimes we present for a Fortune 500 company with a customized keynote, occasionally a fun high school or college show with a motivational message, a fundraiser for a local community in rural areas to a group of billionaires seeking understanding of the mind. Even physicians or HCP's (Health Care Professionals) with interest to understand how hypnosis can enhance their relationships with their patients. As with the people being so varied, the message within the performance is always different, intriguing, fun and interesting.

I remember an event with handwriting specialist doing a study to understand how handwriting can determine the subconscious traits of individuals under a trance. This was an elite group of specialists who worked with the FBI and other agencies as they were experts in determining the profiling of suspects via analysis of handwriting samples.

We regressed individuals to famous murder suspects, Albert Einstein, children who had loving parents, children who hated their parents to a teenager that was in love. The study was used as a baseline to compare and confirm the accuracy of handwriting traits of profiled types. It was interesting to see how anyone under trance could reveal certain characteristic aspects of the handwriting of profiled individual types via deliberate suggestion to the subconscious.

Overall, people are intrigued when they experience a demonstration of the power of the mind, especially after seeing the hypnosis demonstration part of our keynote. We can discuss the mind in many ways, but when the audience gets a chance to witness firsthand the power of hypnosis, the process opens up the covert need for deep understanding.

After events, people come up to me and ask me about meditation, mindfulness and some about the power of attraction. It seems that many are seeking answers on how to take control of their mind or how to inject happiness into their lives. Sometimes all that is needed a is a shift in their perception of their reality. This shift is mostly a subconscious process.

Some ask how they can get motivated and stay motivated. Some mention that they've always wanted to learn more about how to control their mind, but no one has ever shown them how. It seems that many are starving for more in-depth understanding of how their mind works.

ADD AND ADHD – ADDICTION TO DISTRACTION?

After a corporate event, I was approached by a couple concerned about their child who was just diagnosed with ADD (Attention Deficit Disorder or ADHD Attention Deficit Hyperactivity Disorder). My comment back to them was to consider that this condition is simply their child is "addicted to distraction." They just looked at me and then each other while reflecting on their child, and fully agreed that this could be the case with their child. Their big concern was that the doctor wanted to put their child on drugs indefinitely.

With the use of cell phones in almost every hand and all the hyperactivity our hi-tech world encompasses it's a worthy concept to consider. Think of the statement mentioned earlier that "We human beings are extremely suggestible creatures" and how we are constantly bombarded with stimulus overload with suggestions coming from every direction.

We are an adapting type of species, and we adapt to constant distraction. When the distraction stops, our minds don't stop and have a time of withdrawal. If we don't understand this process is happening, we might seek to add more distraction to ease the uneasiness of a un-distracted (calm) mind – "addiction."

I've had several opportunities to share some time and consult with several young adults who were seeking ways to relieve this hyper-activity of their mind. Sometimes parents would have me speak to their child with them after a show. I would coach these kids and help them regain control of their mind by simply understanding and using the meditation technique that we offer. After using the meditation for various periods of time, the results I have seen have been wonderful. I wouldn't call these clinical studies, but real field cases that I have encountered that always offer relief and change of perspective.

Chapter 26

STRESS IS HYPNOSIS

*"Life is ten percent what you experience
and ninety percent how you respond to it."*

~ Dorothy M. Neddermeyer PHD

*Breaking free from stresses hypnotic influence
and its negative effects on your health*

We all are subject to stress, but we can learn how to not react to it especially when it has the potential to cause us unnecessary upset. By understanding how easily we become hypnotized by our reactions to stress, we can increase our ability to minimize the negative influence it has on our mind and therefore our body. Exercising the muscle of your mind to stay aware as you walk through the pressures of life will help anyone reduce how stress affects your being. The exercise is meditation.

Recent studies I read from the American Psychological Association about stress in America have revealed that with the lifestyles that the average working person or housewife (or househusband), have increased over the years. Stress over time can affect our mind, body, and soul and can have adverse effects that could lead to serious ills, including heart disease, depression, anxiety, and diabetes to name a few. We all have different responses to stress and this stress effects each our bodies in different ways.

WHAT IS STRESS AND LET'S RELATE THIS TO HYPNOSIS AND OUR HEALTH

FACTS ABOUT STRESS:

- Too much stress can result in physical problems, like heart disease, chest pains, high blood pressure to mention just a few.

- Stress changes the neuro-chemical makeup of the body. Just like a placebo has its power in the belief, our perceptual reactions to stress can have negative effects on our bodies function.

- Stress can lead to premature aging and hair loss.

The truth is, this list can go and on, but for now you can see the point.

The bottom line here for our discussion is that beyond the negative physical effects upon our bodies, stress robs our ability to simply have joy and happiness in our daily moments that we encounter day to day.

FACTS ABOUT HYPNOSIS:

- Hypnosis is a natural state of mind that happens to everyone every day.

- Hypnosis is becoming subject to that which you react to.

- Hypnosis is suggestion accepted.

- Hypnosis is when a suggestion bypasses the critical factor of the conscious mind and is accepted by the subconscious.

- Suggestion tends to enter the subconscious mind more efficiently (good or bad) when emotion accompanies the suggestion.

When somebody or something can get you upset, this reaction has emotion attached to it which opens the door to your subconscious. What you react to gets into the subconscious, and therefore in a sense, you are hypnotized by that person or that situation. Once it gets on the inside, it talks to you inside your mind.

When you're dealing with people, you must understand you're not necessarily dealing with that person as much as what has gotten inside their head pulling their strings.

Same thing with a coil of wire as an example. If you have identical coils of wire. One has an electrical charge and the other doesn't, bring them close together and one picks up the charge from the other.

Have you ever noticed when someone could walk into a room with negative energy and how that force can bring the whole room down? In the same way, a positive presence can bring the whole room up.

The world is a tough place full of pressures and stresses that always is testing the armor of our conscious and subconscious mind and tempting us to react. If we could learn the tool of non-reaction at a young age, we would be able to protect ourselves as we go through the many trials that attempt to break down our mind's armor as we go through life. We ultimately learn to grow from stress, but too much stress often has negative effects on our life and health.

When you've trained your mind not to react, you can stay mindful when a negative emotion from a situation or a person tempts you to respond. As you learn the option to switch to a mindfulness state in an instant, you then will be able to listen to the words coming from their mouth and hear the words as a noise with no emotional meaning that has the power to affect you. Let in the good things in life and learn to let the bad things roll off you like the water off a duck's back.

By keeping a barbed wire fence around your mind, as Shivapuri Baba had mentioned in our last section, you will not only be better able to keep your focus on your Godly purpose, but you will be protecting your health and also giving a strong example to those in your life that you would wish to influence positively.

HOW TO "NOT REACT" TO SOMEONE WHEN YOU KNOW THEY MIGHT GET YOU UPSET?

The meditation exercise we teach has the purpose to help you remember to shift to a mindful state when necessary. While doing the meditation process, you are practicing that split second recognition of becoming aware in an instant every time you notice you are not aware. In practice, this would help you step out of potential rabbit holes of the mind before falling in too deep. Once in deep, it is hard to know the difference, as then, you become overcome with the illusions in your minds interpretations of the experience.

A COUPLE OF EXAMPLES OF HOW TO STAY AWARE IN EVERYDAY EXPERIENCES:

Have you ever been on the phone with someone and somehow you engage emotionally and you end up getting upset or into an argument? Next time you are in a situation where you know the call could be a tough encounter, as you feel the anxiety build, simply remember to take the speaker away from your ear about three to four inches. As soon as you do this, you'll now hear the voice on the other end, but it will be reduced to a quieter sound in the distance and not "in your head." This trick will help you become more objective and give you the power to stay mindful and not react from an emotional response, but instead of reason.

A similar effect is when you are watching TV, and you realize that without notice, you are watching a commercial. You might even forget that the commercial began. Instantly, hit the "mute" button on the remote and notice, suddenly, you'll hear the quiet and easily re-engage back to the moment. Remembering to hit the mute button is like remembering to switch to a mindful state in a moment – hence, using your Visionary Mind Power.

When a stressful encounter un-expectedly confronts you, try to remember to be in the room you are in. Start to notice the sounds, the tingling in your hand, the sunlight streaming through the window. Whatever reminds you to be mindful, will be your greatest defense and prevent your energy (awareness) to be taken from you.

Chapter 27

HYPNOTIC INFLUENCE

*"The greatest discovery of my
generation is that a human being can alter
his life by altering his attitudes of mind."*

~ William James

How it can hurt you?

How it can help you?

*Why understanding how it works
can protect you and your loved ones
from being influenced negatively.*

The subconscious mind doesn't have discretion and often picks up suggestions from the world that can be good or bad. How many times have you purchased an item that you didn't need and later regretted buying? Advertisements and media are powerful tools that can subconsciously convince you to purchase something for no real good reason. In subtle ways, the emotion connected to the advertisement along with constant repetition helps to break the message into your subconscious.

Advertisers spend billions of dollars every year to program ideas into our subconscious. If you don't continually work on planting seeds of your ultimate visions of yourself, others will apparently do it for you to their benefit.

Assuming you are a bit older, try to fill in the last phrase for each statement below:

1. Winston Taste Good Like a _____.

2. Please Don't Squeeze the _____.

3. Fly the Friendly Skies of _____.

4. You're in Good Hands with _____.

If you're a bit younger, you may respond more readily to:

5. MacDonald's Says _____.

6. Nike Says _____.

7. What Motel Leaves the Lights On? _____.

8. It Melts in Your Mouth Not _____.

Answers in order:

1. Cigarette Should.
2. Charmin.
3. United.
4. Allstate.
5. I'm Lovin' It!
6. Just Do It.
7. Motel 6.
8. In Your Hand.

The point is that we didn't try to remember these commercials, yet these ads are foremost in our minds after all the years have passed. Advertisers spend large amounts of money to influence the masses subconscious. They know that when making a decision to buy the products or services, the chances of remembering these brands will be greater in many individuals when making a buying decision.

This process of programming occurs throughout our lives and continually influences our subconscious in countless ways – good or bad. To reiterate, by understanding how to use our Visionary Mind Power, we can begin to control how these unconscious influences affect us and become more conscious of what we accept and let into our minds.

Thought: Think how the news media influences the masses in various and countless ways. This very well could be the cornerstone of the division we find in our country. As each person watches their same station or social media source – good or bad – continuously, many become unconsciously influenced in various ways depending on their perception and suggestibility. This process is happening all the time more than ever in our human history creating countless conflicting views.

HOW IT CAN HURT YOU?

In the same way, we often have programmed limiting beliefs from our reactions to our parents, teachers, siblings or any form of bullying in early stages of our lives. Here are a couple of examples of negative parenting or early life influences.

Think of the child who keeps hearing the suggestion from his mother, scolding with emotion, "You're going to be just like your father, you're going to be just like your father..."

The mother later forgets her suggestion that she gives the child and goes on in her life. The child holds on to the suggestion that was charged with emotion, and becomes just like his father or rebels and does the opposite actions in life to compensate to not be like his father. Either way, he is influenced by the suggestion that filters into his subconscious mind by constant repetition along with the emotion felt by the mother.

Another limiting belief many children pick up from their parents or peers from a young age is the limiting belief of their potential. This could manifest in many ways.

Parents sometimes make a young child believe that they "can't" do this or that at an early age. The first word a child learns is often the word "no." Most of the base learning of a human occurs in early childhood. This is a time when we are in the early stages of growth where we are learning pattern of thinking and doing that become routines that develop into habits that define who we are.

The child risks holding onto these suggestions and is affected by them in the later years of life. This specific type of conditioning might limit the growing adult by feeling he (or she) can't move forward to pursue his or her dreams fearing this pursuit will be shot down. This remnant suggestion might limit the motivating force necessary to succeed by simply creating the fear to take the first step necessary to pursue any goals or make any transformational change.

HOW IT CAN HELP YOU?

The ways that we get influenced negatively can go on and on. The message here is that we don't even consider that we've been influenced, until we realize we have some type of subtle resentment that generally is an indicator. One day the grown child might see that he or she was influenced by their parents or peers, and from here, is able to consciously change their motivations and hang ups with conscious choice.

The healing might happen first when the child (now growing into an adult) allows himself to realize the mom, dad, older brother, sister or any other influence, didn't know what they were doing and is forgiven – at least in the mind. At this juncture one can begin to forgive and forget and make mental adjustments to get back on the path that has heart for them.

These early suggestions are so deeply rooted in the subconscious that it's hard to detect. This built in self defeating mechanism **MUST** be overcome to open oneself to life's limitless positive creating potential.

BREAKING THE CHAINS OF PAST GENERATIONS

Understanding how easily we are influenced at a young age or in any relationship as one grows up, can help any adult realize how placing your will onto anyone over and over can create an inordinate influence. Wouldn't it make sense to be a force of empowerment rather that a negative influence creating hang-ups that others will grow to resent you for in the future.

Please don't misunderstand, there is certainly a time any of us can use constructive criticism. I always admired those who have the strength to give me good advise so I am able to see myself. When someone disagrees with integrity versus disagreeing with a disagreeable attitude, the former has a more natural corrective force.

When one can learn to see undesirable aspects of themselves, affirmations and new visions can now be created that consciously can influence the subconscious mind. When you are able to understand how to re-program yourself away from unconscious bad influences you picked up earlier in your life, you might then also see how you might be unconsciously imposing your will upon those that you influence. By seeing this, you can break the chains to the unnecessary bad habits of past generations. A great example of this is within a story I once heard.

There was a woman who was telling her daughter how to make a pot roast. Among other things, she told her to cut the ends of the roast off before placing into the pot, before going into the oven. One day the daughter asked the mom, "Why are we cutting the ends of the roast off?" The mother explained that her mother had told her to do that. Finally the mother and daughter were able to visit the grandmother. When she was asked the question of, "Why are we suppose to cut the ends of the roast off before placing in the pot?" The grandmother simply said, "so the roast will fit into the pot!"

Chapter 28

THE POWER OF PURPOSE

*"When you are inspired by some great purpose, some
extraordinary project, all your thoughts break their bonds:
Your mind transcends limitations, your consciousness expands
in every direction, and you find yourself in a new, great, and
wonderful world. Dormant forces, faculties and talents become
alive, and you discover yourself to be a greater person by
far than you ever dreamed yourself to be."*

~ Patanjali

It's important to reiterate and drive the following point home. The
one thing we all have in common is the ability to control the
thoughts that pass through our minds. These thoughts help mold
our perception that dictates our experience. This is within our
inherent capability of free will, and from this premise all man is
created equal.

The truth is that we either don't usually use this ability or don't
know the secret (technique) of how to master our thoughts and
change their content that ultimate influence our subconscious.

When we learn the secret of mastering our thoughts, we will learn to "change our lives" in any direction we choose and truly use our Visionary Mind Power.

LEVERAGE PURPOSE FOR CHANGE

There have been many powerful books that have inspired the masses. One in particular is "Man's Search for Meaning," written by Dr. Frankel (1905-1997) who wrote of his experiences as a prisoner surviving a German concentration camp. He witnessed misery and death all around him. In the midst of what appeared as a hopeless situation, he knew he needed to survive so he could teach the world, to prevent that this would never happen again (goal – purpose). He realized, through his own observation of those imprisoned, who thought that this was their end, and as a result lost hope, eventually died at the concentration camp. His knowing that he had to live to fulfill his purpose helped him survive through the unthinkable wrath.

There are ways you can leverage a purpose behind making any change you find important for you. a few examples:

1.

Problem: You want to stop smoking but have no motivation to do so.

Leverage: You want to be a positive example for your children so they see a strong positive influence from their parent – purpose.

2.

Problem: Your health is at risk because of lack of exercise and bad eating habits.

Leverage: You decide that you want to change your lifestyle so you have the chance to live a longer life to see your grandchildren grow up and witness them getting married – motivation for change.

3.

Problem: You're not happy with your job and not making enough money to live they way you feel you deserve.

Leverage: You see that education is important to get a better job opportunity and you decide you'll be happier seeking the job you feel that allows you to make more money and express your passion. Now you have purpose and drive to do what you need to do to get where you want to go.

The point is that whatever motivation you choose to help you leverage change is your motivation and perception that works for you. It could just be a personal quest to be a better person and be more connected to the path that has heart for you.

Chapter 29

THE POWER OF FAITH

"The only way you're going to reach places you've never gone is if you trust God's direction to do things you've never done."

~ Germany Kent

The thoughts we allow into our consciousness become what we are able to perceive and believe in our minds – good or bad. As the bible says, "Faith is the assured expectations of things hoped for." With faith, a mental ideology where impossibilities are seen as possible, challenges that are "hopeless" and "unconquerable" are seen as possible.

Think of Albert Einstein who practiced what he called his "thought experiments." He would take time everyday to visualize anything he wanted greater insight into. In one of these experiments he would imagine and visualize what it was like to ride alongside a beam of light. At age 16, he did this experimentation every day. Einstein's habits of repetition of using his Visionary Mind Power eventually helped him manifest insight that helped him develop various laws and principals to solve problems that truly changed the world as we know it.

By doing your own "thought experiments," about any situation that you would like to see happen will help you develop insight that ultimately will lead to faith. Faith will give you confidence and natural motivation as you begin to build a detailed picture of the final outcome. The apparent actions to accomplish, or opportunities to act upon, will now more easily be noticed. You'll find it easier to resist the temptation to give into doubt and worry, as in the back of your mind you have established a mental picture of the final outcome. Visionary Mind Power.

Action: Planting the seed of "faith". Think of the ideal you and create and build a mental picture of who you see yourself to be as if it's already happened. Think of this idea of who you ideally want to be. Think of this vision often and dream your ideal you into your reality. From there, you'll see clearly what you need to do to get where you want to go and the process will seem natural, joyful and fun.

This is why we need to define, write down and understand our goals. By constantly reflecting and updating our goals and visions, we are able to build our vision on paper and in our minds. This repetition, over and over again, is like planting seeds into the figurative garden of our subconscious mind.

Action for getting and keeping motivated: After writing down your goals over and over again and detailing them, then simply edit it onto a five minute reading that can be recorded on your phone or a CD to be played over and over again. The more you listen to the recording the better. Even if you play it while focusing on other things, your subconscious will be influenced nonetheless. Don't forget to update the recording as you gain more insight. Don't delay and write down your new insights as they come to you, this is your gift and result of your own personal "thought experiment."

Like we stated, advertisers spend billions to influence your subconscious via repetition whether you consciously listen to the ads or not. Why not use this same technique for your own visions of your life? The repetition of thoughts over and over again eventually will create a feeling of faith. The seeds in our mind's garden will begin to germinate. Faith that our goals are obtainable will help one see the necessary actions to be taken to manifest what we want to happen. We need to visualize as if it has already happened. This is why we often become what we believe – good or bad.

Chapter 30

HYPNOSIS OF LIMITING BELIEF

"Chronic self-doubt is a symptom of the core belief,
'I'm not good enough.' We adopt these types of limiting
beliefs in response to our family and childhood experiences,
and they become rooted in the subconscious… we have
the ability to take action to override it…"

~ Lauren Mackler

I think of a baby elephant at a circus. The animal keepers tie the young large creature to a stake with a rope. It grows up, and nevertheless, they tie it to the same stake. They may not even tie the rope tighter or make the stake stronger, as they don't need to. Although the elephant grows up and becomes larger and stronger and could easily pull the stake out of the ground, it doesn't go anywhere because it doesn't know it can. The elephant doesn't understand it's potential and therefore accepts this limiting belief.

Put some flies into a jar with a screen on top. Provide food and water and leave them in the jar for a couple of weeks. Take the screen off the jar, the flies will stay in the jar as they, for the moment, have accepted their limitation of possibilities.

We've all had a fly in our car at one time or another. You get in and see the fly that emerges as you start your car. You open the window and offer him his freedom. You can't get him to fly out. You don't want to kill him, but offer him his freedom as you literally try to fan him out of an open window.

It's the same thing as the previous example. As you are going about your day to day business, that fly is contained within the confines of the car and learns and accepts it's limitations of the clear glass becoming an impassible barrier – whether the window is open or not. Eventually the fly will explore the open window area and realize the barrier is passable.

If the fly can eventually learn to transcend this limitation, so it is the same for us human beings and our learned limiting beliefs. We are creatures of learned habit – good or bad. Life's day to day patterns of living have the same affect on limiting our beliefs. I keep saying – good or bad – because I want to drive the point home, that we have free will. We always have choices that are right in front of us, but we often are so set in our ways that we have "learned" to accept our limiting beliefs and habitually blind ourselves to the unlimited possibilities sitting right in front of us.

How many times have you ran into a person, asking, "How are you doing?" The common response "Same ole', same ole' " is a continuous suggestion that will keep anyone in the "Same old situation day in and day out for a lifetime."

The tragedy in this is that when people say this, often I feel the pain – deep down. The pain that they've unconsciously accepted that they have limited themselves from being childlike creative expressions of God. The worlds day to day habitual patterns have swallowed up their ability to be simple, innocent and inspired examples of spirit expressing and fulfilling its purpose. This stifling, I believe, advances the aging process and robs us of the natural process of advancing to a ripe old age fulfilled with wisdom and deep happiness. To creatively express oneself as one advances in age is the most fulfilling purposeful experience one can do and can be accomplished in unlimited ways.

It is said that the average person has approximately 65,000 thoughts that pass through the mind every day. Often, these thoughts repeat themselves day after day, manifesting the same view of reality, attracting the same things to our lives again and again (hence, "same ol', same ol' "). This is the Law of Attraction at work. This is why when you "struggle to overcome your problems", the problems persist. The Law of Attraction keeps attracting you to the "mindset" you're trying to overcome.

Although we have control of our "conscious minds," (or so we think!), we often are not aware of how our subconscious is being influenced. It is our subconscious mind that is the engine facilitating many of our actions.

You may recall times when you have thought to yourself, "Where did that idea, thought, comment or action come from?" Why not have all these spontaneous actions, thoughts and perceptions be fully focused around the life and ideals that "you" have dreamed to manifest.

The process of self hypnosis is how real change can happen with little effort on your part. So, like driving home in a trance, (forgetting that you are driving, and yet still always moving towards your final destination – home) you can move towards your goals without any effort or conscious awareness on your part.

ANALOGIES OF THE MIND

And now, once again back to the computer as an example as a way to increase the insight into the point to follow.

Our subconscious mind is an immense area of stored information with infinite intelligence. If the mind were compared to a computer, the subconscious would be our hard drive and our conscious mind would be our RAM – random access memory. Our senses perceive and gather information continuously either from our "conscious" thoughts or influences from outside suggestions. These perceptual "interpretations" continually influence our subconscious mind.

As we pick up stimuli from our senses, we unconsciously interpret more information than our conscious minds (RAM) can perceive. Our subconscious mind absorbs and stores desirable and undesirable information continuously whether we are aware of this or not. This information sneaks past the conscious mind as it doesn't get a chance to use its discretion. Like a virus that sneaks undetected into your computer, unwanted suggestions (unconscious thoughts, beliefs and ideas that are taken as subtle commands) become stored into our subconscious and influence our conscious perceptions of our reality.

If our mind were represented by an iceberg, our vast subconscious would be 95% below the surface and our conscious mind above. We need to use the 5% of our conscious mind (surface mind) to "consciously" influence and tap into our greater subconscious (mind below).

When the seed of suggestion is planted into our subconscious mind, it is as if our subconscious is like the soil (beneath the ground where roots take hold). If this truth has merit, would it not be wise to "consciously" plant as many good seeds as possible until these seeds take root and thereby dominate the subconscious mind, and thereby, it's influence of the conscious mind?

The seed will take root and keep growing underneath the soil and at various times rise to the surface. The suggestions planted into the subconscious mind unconsciously keep reminding the conscious mind of what it needs to do or think.

A truly negative example of this is PTSS for soldiers that have relapsed months or years after the incident that caused them emotional strife. We all are soldiers walking through the battlefield of life. If we can learn to walk through our experiences with mindfulness, we can limit and be in command of the negative seeds that attempt to root into our subconscious – Visionary Mind Power.

Chapter 31

WHAT IS THE LAW OF ATTRACTION?

"Imagination is everything.
It is the preview of life's coming attractions."

~ Albert Einstein

HOW DOES IT WORK?

"Be thankful for what you have, you'll end up having more.
If you concentrate on what you don't have,
you will never ever have enough."

~ Oprah Winfrey

WHY DOES IT WORK?

"Man, alone, has the power to transform
his thoughts into physical reality;
man, alone, can dream and make
his dreams come true."

~ Napoleon Hill

Some mention that they have seen the movie "The Secret" and didn't know how to do what the movie suggests that anyone can do. The movie teaches the concept of the Power of Attraction. The idea centers around the fact that what you focus your mind on continually will eventually manifest in your life. Unfortunately, "The Secret" does tell you what you need to do, but it doesn't necessarily tell you how to use the powerful tool of your mind to manifest the powerful changes that many yearn to occur in their lives. It is my goal in this book to convey the "how to."

Before you ever thought about the car you drive, you rarely noticed it on the road. Once you finished your research and made a decision to buy the car you now drive, you accepted this car into your subconscious at the same time. The color, the year, the make and model are foremost in your subconscious mind.

An interesting phenomenon occurs when driving your new car. You begin to notice your "same car" on the road, more than you ever noticed before. You easily recognize the same make, model, and color and may exclaim to yourself, "everyone's driving the same car!" You notice that which you have – in your subconscious. So, in the same way, the Power of Attraction works.

Understanding and accepting the concept that we are creatures of habit, and seeing that we are subject to some level of trance in our everyday life, opens the door to see positive change in thought, and therefore perception, becomes possible. The meditation techniques we teach has the objective to help one to understand how to become objective to the mind's thought processes. Once this process is followed, one can begin to build a strong mind by exercising their ability to become "aware" and choose how we allow our subconscious to be influenced.

Once "aware," you will begin to understand the "how to" for changing unwanted thoughts to desirable ones. This is the most important component to using the mind to manifest the magic of Power of Attraction into your life. This is about learning to use this magic to manifest visions and desired outcomes beyond the limited expectations of your life. As your ability to shift your perception is mastered, you will be able to use self-hypnosis in very specific and powerful ways.

Action: Consciously write down and continually repeat and visualize all that you want to be in your life and let this build in your imagination. Do this daily. Doing this more often will multiply the effectiveness of this powerful technique.

Once your visions become strong and real to you, the magic of the universe will allow you to have the faith that enables you to see your visions as a real possibility. The more detailed the picture of your vision the more deeply you can influence your subconscious. Think of the statement: "A picture is worth a thousand words." From here, you'll begin to notice the things you need to act upon that pop up in life to help manifest your vision. You then will be able to recognize the actions necessary to move towards these outcomes. Hence, the Power of Attraction.

Chapter 32

HYPNOSIS AND NLP

*"We can't solve problems using the same type
of thinking we used when we created them."*

~ Albert Einstein

Hypnosis is a great tool and can be utilized with an understanding of Neuro-Linguistic Programming (NLP). NLP is a technique
that is well used within self-hypnosis and important to understand
for anyone seeking any level of self-transformation.

In its simplest terms:

Neuro is the way we process information received from our
senses – seeing, tasting, smelling, hearing and touching.

Linguistic is the way we perceive and internalize the world
based on the information we receive from our experiences.

Programming is how we code the information to create the
habits, memories, and actions.

Back to thinking of our mind to be like a computer. The computer itself is the hardware – the mind. The software on a computer is loaded into a new computer and determines the way we process the information that is "entered" into the machine. For us, the software is often a "habit" of dealing with the things of life (good or bad). The results and the outcome is the result of these programming processes.

We merely need to take the information we receive through our senses – **neuro**, then process – **linguistic** – and store this information in a certain way to create a desired point of view that ultimately leads us to a desirable result – **programming**.

With the computer, we choose how the information is processed to get the results we want. With our minds, however, sometimes the information we receive is processed in a way that creates undesirable results – old habits of processing information.

The process of NLP would be to upgrade the software in our minds so we can change the way we process our experiences within the computer of our mind and manipulate incoming information "preferably" to get the desired reaction that influences our subconscious. This sequence of actions is paramount in creating the life that we want by upgrading bad habits to good habits and have them integrate into our lives.

THE NLP PROCESS – A SIMPLE APPLICATION

The first thing to do is to understand where you are now. Sit back and think "why did I process that information the way I did, causing these undesirable outcomes."

Slow your reading down again and feel each of the words individually and give it a try.

To start, It would be helpful to:

See yourself from a distant place, as if you were in a movie theater watching the screen of your life.

Quiet your mind, then use your imagination and build a vision of the undesirable you (an aspect of you that you would prefer to change). Contemplate the totality of the vision of the way you are now. Feel everything about it that you don't like and hope to change.

Then, place this whole vision aside and create a new vision on a different screen in your mind.

Build an objective view of the way other people successfully have taken the same conditions and created desirable outcomes. Study the way they did things, the way they processed their information, try to visualize how they feel, what they did differently, their habits of success, and now compare this to how you feel yourself on your initial screen. What did they do differently?

Now take the feelings from the second screen and build a new vision of yourself on the first movie screen in your mind. See yourself doing and feeling differently. Create a new unique opportunity in your mind. Imagine. Dream. You are now creating a new possibility in your mind for yourself using NLP. Next time the same situation presents itself, you now have

a better chance of recognizing a "choice" that you hadn't considered in the past.

Perhaps the only difference with successful people is the way they processed failure. They understood that there is no such thing as failure, only feedback giving powerful lessons to teach you what you need to do to reach your desired outcomes. This way when you consider what you thought to be a failure, you learn to understand this as a simple stepping stone to help you advance towards your success.

Just know that if someone else can do something, then so can you.

The "meditation" sets the stage to help one strengthen their ability and insight into recognizing undesirable thoughts and changing them into desirable ones.

By quieting your mind of all preconceived perceptions, you are now opening the door to allowing your "creative imagination" to feed you new possibilities.

"Hypnosis" with an understanding of "NLP" is a resource you can use to increase your ability to reprogram your mind with new ideas and beliefs. As you learn to modify the software of your mind, you will learn the secret of processing information differently so your view of your experiences will become desirable and lead you on your path of excellence! Integrating all "these powerful mind tools" together to manifest beyond your own perceived limitations is utilizing your Visionary Mind Power – VMP.

Note: You can never fail if you don't give up. One needs to understand perceived failure as a simple lesson showing you the way that doesn't work.

Chapter 33

THINKING BEYOND HABITUAL THINKING

It's often hard to see our bad habits
and gain awareness of better habits

You may feel that something isn't right with your process of life, but you also realize that you don't understand the change you need to consider for yourself. Often, it's hard to **"think outside your habitual thinking"** and need to see beyond limiting habitual thought processes to identify what changes need to be made in the first place.

Like Albert Einstein said:

We can't solve problems
using the same type of thinking
we used when we created them.

We need to study the **"positive deviant"** to help us identify less useful habits that don't serve us well that might be difficult to see in oneself.

The positive deviant: Someone within any circumstance in life who given the same conditions somehow perform outstandingly greater than others in an observed group. We study and try to understand what these people are doing differently. They may not be working that much harder, but consistently outperform the others with specific "habits" that we hope to implement in ourselves.

These positive deviants have habits. As mentioned earlier, we are creatures of habits good or bad.

Good habits are great as they make your life more efficient.

Bad habits tend to bring undesirable conditions forth in our lives as we continue to do things that simply do not serve us well. Perhaps at one time these "bad habits" were useful and perhaps even "good habits" at one time, but they obviously have become obsolete, and the option to change something about "the way we do things, or how we think" becomes apparent for a more positive experience.

As mentioned above, sometimes it's hard to know how to process your perceptions differently when you already have a "tendency" that is hard for yourself to see. When mentioning the idea of studying how successful people have persevered, let's go into this with some specific examples. This concept is from a business seminar, but can easily be applied to our personal lives as well.

During our keynote presentations within our corporate seminars, we discuss much of the principals of the mind focused on any theme derived from a needs assessment questionnaire and inter-view with company management or board members before the event. Each event is focused on Visionary Mind Power and the importance of understanding how to influence the subconscious mind positively. If the message were to increase productivity or increase sales, we would often study the positive deviant.

By noting the effective habits the positive deviants have that reflect their outstanding performance, we can begin to understand the unproductive habits that others may have that don't work to their advantage to keep competitive. Once we recognize the good effective habits, we discuss methods that can be used to modify less effective habits to increase productivity. Among other techniques to adopt change, I do a fun hypnosis demonstration on stage to reveal the power of hypnosis to create new habits on a subconscious level.

A few simple examples of a positive deviant's habit for success in sales would be to:

1. Ask for referrals to all your existing clients in the course of business interactions. This simple habit that doesn't take too much time and energy timed correctly within normal business interactions with clients could be the simple practice that could increase sales 100% or more.

2. Another effective habit revealed in studying the positive deviant in a sales seminar was that we noticed they had the habit of making ten new calls a day. This good habit only took 30 to 45 minutes but was the main reason the positive deviant was the top producer sometimes creating triple the sales from the average. We noted the habit was to simply create the ten leads to call before leaving the office at the end of the day, and then making the calls first thing in the morning. The positive deviants didn't need to think, just follow this simple habit that brought outstanding success. Indeed a subconscious process.

HABITS OF HEALTHY AND UNHEALTHY

What about simply the good habits of the most healthy. Healthcare is one of the greatest costs for an individual or a company; it would make sense to reduce this costs however possible.

For two reasons;

1. It would save money if people did preventive measures with good habits to keep healthy.

2. Who would argue that being healthy is always a positive foundation considering the prosperity and happiness in anyone's life?.

If you take 5000 people and note their health conditions, you would find 2 or 3% (100 to 150 people) that have excellent health – positive deviants. You might find that many would not be overweight, they typically didn't call in sick or need to see a doctor much and had more energy than most.

What do these "positive deviants" do to stay so healthy? One might observe that they were attracted to healthy foods, exercise and they meditated to name a few traits.

If you study the "habits of the most unhealthy," one might note the lack of exercise, unhealthy food and eating habits with no outlets to reduce the adverse effects of stress.

Message: The essence of the message here is to find someone that you know personally or in the world when you can say, "I like where this person is coming from and how they have accomplished what they have done." Study them and try to see what they are doing day to day in their process of life, so you may "notice" what they are doing differently than you, that helped them accomplish their success. They may not be working much harder, but they have certain "habits" that work well for them. These are the habits that you can emulate for yourself.

This observation will help you see "what you are doing or not doing," which then will help you put into practice and develop "new habits" for yourself to help you facilitate to get where you want to be in life. As with any excursion, the journey starts by understanding where you are now and where you want to go. Then, all one needs to do is make a "conscious" plan on how to get there.

Thought: Just think if a program could be in place that could effectively influence the habits of just 10% of the people in our sample, that would be over 800 people that could benefit from these positive, healthy habits.

Note: These are simple examples, but the point is, as noted already in past chapters, we gain habits unconsciously good or bad by how we are influenced along with the simple repetition of an action or pattern of processing life experiences. Once we recognize what we need to change, we can use 1 – Repetition, 2 – NLP or 3 – (Self) hypnosis to get these new habits into our subconscious.

Chapter 34

THE POWER OF SUGGESTION

… for healing and influencing.

Why it's important for anyone to understand hypnosis.

*"I survived because the fire inside me
burned brighterthan the fire around me."*

~ Joshua Graham

It is time to take a deep breath and capture the moment.

**Right now, as you're reading this, slow down –
be in the room and slowly read the following:**

**Read and feel each word and use your creative
imagination.**

Imagine a lemon. See it in your mind.

A ripe, juicy lemon. Smell it if you can.

A lemon is a fruit, not like an apple or an orange.

We don't eat a lemon as it makes your mouth water and pucker.

Now imagine the lemon being cut in half.

Imagine the sweet and sour smell of lemon.

Smell the juices as they get on your hand and you bring it towards your mouth.

Feel what it would feel like to take that lemon and bite into it making your mouth pucker with the sour yet sweet acidic taste.

See in your mind someone taking a bite of the lemon as you see their mouth pucker in reaction to the bitterness.

Is your mouth now salivating?

During a stage-hypnosis show when I describe this scenario, typically over 70% of the crowd says "yes to having their mouth water." In a matter of seconds, this simple suggestion was able to create a biophysical reaction to many in a crowd. If this physical effect occurs with this simple implication, can you imagine the power your thoughts have on the healing process? Or the disease (dis-ease with your environment – stress) process?

As mentioned earlier, in the movie "What the Bleep Do You K(now)!" the documentary explains the connection between thought patterns and the minds ability to take outside stimuli, interpret them within and create biophysical reactions based on an individual's perception. A response to anything on the outside that is interpreted for hunger, sex, anger or any other emotional reaction, releases instantly throughout the body very powerful peptides that arouse emotion and affect the whole body physically on a cellular level. A compelling movie with an important message that I suggest you get and watch several times.

As with the lemon effect above and considering the power of placebo, if you can believe and imagine in your mind that you can heal your illness or injury, your body will attempt to manufacture a remedy that can heal your body. I'm not a doctor, nor am I suggesting that one should discontinue the use of any prescribed drug or recommendation from a doctor, but never underestimate the power of your mind's ability to help heal your body's disease, illness, and injury.

Truly your body is healing itself all the time. The fact that you are here today is proof that your body has been healing, improving and regenerating itself your whole life.

Taking a deeper look, you can see how negative thought patterns derived from stress and worry can indeed cause your body to react and may reduce immune system functions or even induce illnesses! To take responsibility for your thoughts and the way you perceive experiences is a powerful way to take control and affect the healing process of your mind, body, and spirit.

Thought to remember: You become what you believe. Learn to master your thoughts, and you will master your life, wellness, and happiness.

WHY IT'S IMPORTANT FOR DOCTORS
TO UNDERSTAND HYPNOSIS?

I recently did a seminar for a group of Health Care Professionals (HCP's) and also a keynote event for an award night for a group of physicians and HCP's at Harvard. The theme for both events was "Why it is important for HCP's to understand hypnosis?"

In customizing the keynote for the HCP audience's, I brought forth the principal of placebo. A placebo is a drug that looks like the real drug but is simply is a sugar pill. Often when drugs are tested by the drug manufacturer, some of the subjects doing the test are given a placebo thinking this is the drug they are testing. The placebo effect is tested against the real drug to determine its effectiveness.

The FDA requires a drug to perform at least a small percentage better than a placebo consistently for a drug manufacturer to advertise specific structure and functional medical claims. So based on this fact, it is known that the "belief" that the drug will help with known symptoms is a huge consideration of the healing process associated with the drug under study.

Let's consider the use of a placebo. The placebo effect states that if you believe that the drug I'm about to give you is the most powerful anti-cold medication available (actually just a sugar pill – placebo), your body will attempt to manufacture the very drug necessary to alleviate the condition. This drug that your body manufactures will be the exact dose your body needs and often more powerful than any pharmaceutical drug and with no side effects. This, of course, is based on the fact that the real drug only needs to be slightly more effective on a consistent basis than the placebo.

I'm not an expert on the placebo effect or understand how the body does this, but I do understand the power of suggestion and do know the power of belief – good or bad. Even drug manufacturers know the power of belief based on the testing of drugs against a placebo, but also know that they can't sell a drug if the consumer knew how to have the right mindset to heal themselves.

Something to think about.

THE POWER OF SUGGESTION FROM A DOCTOR OR HCP

Given the fact that a patient is given a drug (or a placebo) from a doctor or health professional and this occurs when studying the effectiveness of a drug. Health professionals and doctors are considered credible therefore anything they give to a patient has built-in expectations on the part of the patient that the drug is going to help them – belief. That being the case, all health professionals must realize they are in effect a hypnotist and should choose their communication wisely as the words they use and actions expressed can create healing expectations for the patient.

I cringe when I hear the story of a doctor telling a patient that he has a month to live and there "is not" a cure. Of course, this could be true, but being in the position they are in, and with a highly suggestible patient, this suggestion could very well be a death sentence for certain people.

We then discussed how HCP's could be more effective using the power of suggestion to enhance the patients healing.

GETTING RAPPORT IS VITAL FOR AN EFFECTIVE SUGGESTION

Developing rapport with whomever you deal with is vital for effective influence. Rapport happens when anyone, in any situation, takes a sincere approach to listen to anyone they confront to the point where the other knows that you hear where they are coming from – getting on the same page.

The more doctors let go of their academic knowledge for a moment and take the time to develop a great rapport with their patients, the greater is the power of suggestion. This suggestion can take the form of the placebo effect with the drugs they prescribe, but more importantly with any change talk they "suggest" to help the patient make the necessary changes to help their health condition.

By giving the healing process back to the patient, the patient once again has the power of healing in their own hands. It is known among doctors that the greatest part of the healing indeed is the from the patient themselves.

RAPPORT IS LISTENING

The principal of getting rapport is a powerful way for anyone to have more effective influence within any interaction. The key here is to listen.

Magic happens when the person you're communicating with, know that you "really hear" that you understand their concerns and feelings about anything. The doorway to influence is now opened up to their subconscious, and they are more open to your suggestion – whatever it is – good or bad.

Think of the times you have visited a doctor. Each of your doctor visits was different. You might have remembered an appointment, as you were talking to the doctor and answering his systematic questions. Meanwhile, he or she was looking at a computer screen as you didn't feel a connection, as to the doctor under-standing "your" real concerns. As a result, you might have been prescribed a drug or therapy and thought, "they're just pushing drugs onto me and extracting money with therapies or possible surgeries that I don't need."

In contrast, you might have had the experience when the doctor sin-cerely took the time to listen to you. Your mind might have jumped to attention when you felt the doctor stopped what he was doing and took the time to look you in the eyes and to let you know, that he or she knew where you were coming from exactly. There was a point when you felt the doctor fully understood your perspective and concerns, as you might have noticed, in that instance, your mind became a little brighter. In that moment, your subconscious was most open to suggestion. When this connection occurs, the doctor has more power to help you help yourself with the drugs he or she prescribes, therapies, or the change talk suggested to you.

This principle of rapport is powerfully effective in many ways when you deal with people in general. It works with your spouse, children, boss, your co-workers, a date or any person you might meet in your day to day interactions.

RAPPORT IN STAGE HYPNOSIS

Getting rapport with a crowd as a stage hypnotist is paramount to successful stage hypnosis. As a stage performer, I always need to think where the crowd is coming from to gain strong rapport. I try to perceive the audience as if they were thinking, "What's in this for me?" From there, any message is better received if I can talk the language pertinent to the audience.

RAPPORT IN HYPNOTHERAPY

When doing hypnotherapy, it's the same thing. Establishing rapport is important to create a successful session. First, it's important to explain clearly to the client the process of hypnosis and how it will help them. Then, it is vitally important to listen to where the client is coming from while getting on the same page as to their "core concerns." From here, the suggestions crafted for the therapy are most effective when leveraged to their foundational needs that will be best received into their subconscious – by resonating strongly to "their" perception.

WE ALL ARE HYPNOTISTS AND WILL BE
MORE EFFECTIVE ESTABLISHING RAPPORT

Within this concept, I encourage you to try to be a better listener. As you naturally learn to practice mindfulness as you walk through life, you will find this sets the stage to open your mind to the perception of where others are coming from. From here, you'll enhance your ability for more effective communication.

RAPPORT IN SELLING

It's the same thing if you are in sales and take your time to listen to the person you're selling to. They will tell you what they need if you just listen.

If you are looking to buy a car and interacting with a salesman, and mention you are seeking a reliable, safe and economical car, yet the salesman keeps saying "this car is fast, you're going to have the hottest car in town," you'll less likely be enticed to buy as your needs are not being heard.

If you establish great rapport by listening to the needs of whomever you're selling to and letting them know that their needs are understood, you'll find it easier and more effective to close deals.

WE ALL ARE HYPNOTISTS AND CAN ENHANCE
OUR COMMUNICATION WITH OTHERS

The more we allow ourselves to listen to whomever we are dealing with and let them "know" that we hear exactly where they're coming from (gain rapport), the more people will open up to us and allow us to better express ourselves, and be heard by them in all communication.

Chapter 35

PERCEPTION IS EVERYTHING

*When you learn to change the way you
look at things, everything changes.*

Have you ever gone to see a movie because someone had told you that you "have to check out this movie … it's fantastic." You go to this movie, and you're watching the first scenes with great expectations that this movie is going to be indeed incredible. And at first, it seems boring. Still, you stay in the theater with great anticipation for the movie to become interesting. While waiting for the movie to improve you start wondering, "When is this going to get better?"

You keep watching, and still, the movie seems boring as you wonder if it might be too late just to walk out and salvage your night and walk into another movie that you had on your favorite list. You still watch hoping for the great transition. Nothing happens. The movie is over, and as you're exiting, you're thinking, "this was the most boring senseless movie ever."

You might wonder, "Why in the world did this person tell you to see the movie in the first place? What did they see in it?" You realize that you wouldn't recommend the movie to anyone because you'd be embarrassed. You feel like you wasted your time and money.

THE POINT

The movie made it into the theaters, so it must have some merit. At the same time, some people like it, some do not. Yet it's the same movie. It's truly your perception that dictates your experience. As in life, if everything is awesome and you feel in your heart that your life is on track and your spirit feels that you are blessed, then, by all means, keep things as they are.

But there could be things about your life that you feel funny about. When your "heart" tells you that something doesn't feel right, perhaps you feel a little pain, it's now time to know that you can change the way you look at things, and when you do, another whole world of perception, and therefore opportunity, will open up to you. Maybe it's how you look at things. Perhaps it's your procedure for dealing with things. It might be the type of people you associate with. It could be your job, your spouse or a decision that you need to make. Whatever it is, it's your perception, and you have more control of it than you think.

But how do we change our perception?

Master the tools this book reveals that can help open your ability to use your Visionary Mind Power.

In essence, becoming more mindful and aware by using the meditation. Now more objective, your ability to recognize bad habits and thought processes, and therefore, opening yourself to see your limiting perceptions and beliefs that have tricked you into believing a lie. When you "consciously" learn that you can change the thoughts you allow to dominate your mind, you'll find that you can begin to positively influence your subconscious – practice of self-hypnosis. From there new realizations will become apparent, leading you to new opportunities and actions that you will notice to act upon in your life – the power of attraction.

The thoughts we have in our mind attract and lead us to the fate we experience in our lives – sometimes this outcome is favorable, and sometimes it's not, we must understand this and remember that we always have a choice of the way we perceive our experiences. The magic of the ability of our mind to manifest greatness and happiness comes into focus as we see the favorable conditions in our lives that begin to show up by simply learning to banish the doubt.

W.C. Henley sums this up with his famous quote, "I am the Master of my Fate; I am the Captain of my Soul." This simply means that we must understand how to control the thoughts that occupy our mind. We must learn to rid ourselves of unwanted thoughts as we steer our mind in the direction of positive outcomes and positive visions by using our Visionary Mind Power. From here, one can thereby recognize opportunities, new ideas and create plans that will move one towards their envisioned goals and ideals.

HOW TO TAP INTO OUR IMAGINATION FOR NEW IDEAS FOR OUR LIVES?

I read a story about Albert Einstein who used the following process to seek answers to problems. He used to sit up holding a cup of water in the dark contemplating a problem. At the moment of sleep, when the cup of water would fall, he would instantly awaken, turn the light on, and then write down the ideas that came to him when he roused himself from his unlimited imaginative world.

Tip: This is why; when you have a hunch that seems to come out of nowhere, recognize the genius in the idea and **write it down**. These very well could be important messages – gifts – to guide you in the right direction in your life.

Chapter 36

MOST ASKED QUESTIONS AND MYTHS ABOUT HYPNOSIS

"Hypnosis is, perhaps, one of the most misunderstood and controversial methods of psychological treatment. The myths and misconceptions that surround hypnotherapy mostly stem from people's ideas about stage hypnotism."

~ Clifford N. Lazarus, PhD

When I saw my first stage hypnotist in college in the early 80's, there was no understanding of hypnosis beyond a theatrical stage event. I volunteered and was quickly dismissed from the stage as I apparently wasn't one of the best volunteers. I watched the rest of the show from the audience and only remember the volunteers becoming monkeys picking bugs from each other's hair.

When I saw another show in the early 90's, the thought came to my mind that this would be a great way to help people understand many of the messages about the power of the mind that I often expressed.

The statement from Clifford N. Lazarus above was the barrier always needed to overcome in a show to assure the audience that what they heard about hypnosis from other stage shows is not necessarily what they were about to experience.

My pre-talk was always geared to reveal the powers of the mind. My goal on stage was never to make fun of the participants, but to have fun with them with the underlying intent to inspire them with the possibilities of the mind and leave them with some compelling positive suggestions.

HYPNOTIC MYTHS

Some people erroneously believe that to be hypnotized you must be weak-willed or have a low IQ. Numerous studies have shown that hypnotizability is completely unrelated to those characteristics. Hypnotizability has nothing to do with gullibility, submissiveness or being weak-willed. In fact, the stronger your will, the better your concentration, the faster and easier you can go into a trance state.

Hypnosis is not witchcraft, manipulation or magic. It is simply a natural state of mind that can be used as a tool that will allow you to tap into the unlimited creative intelligence of your mind for a positive lasting change.

WHAT NEEDS TO BE UNDERSTOOD TO GET BETTER RESULTS?

Before a hypnosis session, either on stage or in private, it's important to explain what hypnosis is, noting how it is a natural state of mind we experience every day in normal activities. This way you will be more inclined to "not struggle" and be more at ease as you simply let the "induction process" happen.

Definition of induction: A process of guided relaxation that allows trance to occur and therefore opens the portals of the mind to create a bypass of the critical factor of reason. From here, the subconscious mind is more susceptible to accept the suggestion.

By recognizing how trance naturally happens every day within normal situations, you will more likely be comfortable with the process and allow suggestions to break through the "critical factor."

Definition of the critical factor: The doorway of the subconscious that protects your mind from taking in all suggestions. You will not likely take on suggestion when your rational mind doesn't accept the idea. Naturally, we have a barbed wire fence around our mind protecting us from the worlds unlimited suggestions and protecting us from change. Our minds tend to feel safe within – good or bad – and fears the thought of change.

So when your conscious mind is busy planning your life ideally, it should understand that lasting change is most effective when one learns to influence the unconscious – consciously.

WHY CAN'T I BE HYPNOTIZED?

When I'm discussing hypnosis and ask how many people feel they can't be hypnotized? Often, there are many who raise their hands and say "I don't think I can be hypnotized!" Some believe that to be hypnotized one has to put forth an effort. Studies have shown that this is also incorrect. Most people who have been hypnotized say that "It just happened!"

When performing my stage show during my pre-talk, I am looking for the people that can fall into a trance the easiest. During the "induction" process of the show, volunteers are dismissed from the stage that doesn't prove to be good hypnotic subjects. After the show when interviewed, they say that they "tried and tried," but were disappointed as they fell out of trance. Like driving and falling into highway hypnosis, it just happens. The nature of hypnosis is that you don't know that it's happening.

For those who are skeptical, yet still fascinated with the "hypnosis concept," I simply suggest that they give a sincere try if they would like to experience the trance state. Often the people that say they cannot be hypnotized become some of the best subjects. Their comments afterward often are, "I wouldn't have believe it unless I experienced it." The end result is always positive, and they thank me for helping them to experience a part of their mind that allowed them to relax in a way they hadn't for years.

Note: The experience of zero stress and complete relaxation is a byproduct of the hypnosis experience. Many who indicated that they are familiar with mediation have said that they thoroughly enjoyed the experience as it gave them greater insight into their meditation practice.

All that is required to be hypnotized is a willingness and the ability to allow your mind to relax.

By now, you can understand that some people can't be hypnotized because they're already under some level of a trance. There is an art to quieting your mind and just letting go of all your preconceptions and "thinking," so your attention can be focused and undisturbed. One needs to break free of the trance they're already subject to before one can begin to allow oneself to experience change of perception. This is why I always use a meditative process to quiet the mind's of people as a base necessary to break through the critical factor of the conscious to reach into the subconscious.

WHY CAN'T I SLEEP? HOW TO USE
SELF-HYPNOSIS TO SLEEP BETTER?

Have you ever "tried" to go to sleep? Your effort will make the act of falling asleep not happen. You end up being a person that is "trying to go to sleep." Your initial unconscious command to your subconscious might have happened at some point before sleep – i.e. "I'm not going to sleep tonight because of …" Various things trigger this command and become a command to your subconscious.

When you know, it's simply time to go to sleep and know sleep will just happen. It comes in due course. It's when you relax and try less, hypnosis just happens! It is just a process of believing in what you want – faith, instead of believing what you don't want – doubt.

When you learn to consciously guide your thoughts and understand the art of self-hypnosis, you can take unwanted suggestions, i.e., "I'm not going to sleep tonight," and turn them into thoughts, i.e., "I'm looking forward to a great night of sleep as sleep is now easy for me." Mastering Visionary Mind Power will enable you to recognize and master conscious thought processes that affect your subconscious as you go about your day to day life.

UNDERSTANDING THE PORTALS THAT OPEN
THE DOORWAY TO YOUR SUBCONSCIOUS

We mostly don't accept new suggestions, unless they come in undetected. Unconscious reactions to life's stress especially when emotion is attached, tends to break through the critical factor.

We each have special portals that awaken emotion and helps to allow suggestion pass the critical factor into the subconscious. Let's reflect back to some examples of how emotion tends to enhance how suggestion becomes accepted into our subconscious.

1. Advertisers typically try to evoke an emotion within an ad campaign to increase how effective the ad is retained in the minds of the viewers that can influence future buying decisions.

2. The bullied gets an emotional reaction from the bully creating his own personal hell and therefore subject to the bully's humiliation into the future.

3. A soldier experiences a traumatic emotional event on the battlefield causing future flashbacks based on certain events triggering a memory of his past horrific experiences.

Within stage group inductions I find it to be more effective to cover a whole variety of emotional stimulus when doing group inductions as it's necessary to reach several types of people all at once. If I am one-on-one with someone, it would be easier to identify one characteristic for an individual in a pre-interview before a hypnosis session. Scent and vibrant colors might work well for one person to open up the portals of their mind, while something more visual like the freedom of flight or the peace found on a mountain top or a beach would open up suggestibility for another.

We are all different and are affected differently from our experiences based on our personal unique perspectives and interpretations of past experience. Some are more visual, some respond better to sound, and others better to the feelings or the emotion behind a suggestion. You naturally will be more suggestible based on the type of person you are and what is most important to you personally, which creates an emotional response. With practice as with anything else, one can improve and master the emotional process that works best to effectively make any changes that you desire.

HOW DO I RECOGNIZE THE TRANCE STATE?

Have you ever found yourself completely immersed in an activity where you are extremely focused, and everything else is excluded from your reality? That is a natural trance state. Here are some common examples of daily hypnosis:

- While at a movie theater and becoming so absorbed in the movie you forget you're even at the theater, only to realize when the lights go on after the movie has ended.

- Reading a book and being so engaged that the scenes of the book become your own experience; you forget you're turning the pages or even hear someone come in and speak to you.

- When you're in a daydream in your mind and for those moments completely forget where you are and don't even hear when someone is trying to talk to you. Until you hear someone say, "Hey, I'm talking to you!"

The list goes on and on. See if you can recognize the trance state occurring as you see people around you absorbed in various levels of trance. Watch them as you notice that they are lost in the theater of their mind. By realizing this phenomenon, you are more likely to understand how to make communication more effective. By remembering that you are reacting to their perception – dream – you will more likely remember to be aware – mindful – and be in command in all situations that you confront.

HAVE I EVER BEEN HYPNOTIZED?

As a person who practices and teaches meditation, I was always intrigued by the power of hypnosis which led me to be trained and certified in hypnotherapy. At a hypnosis training session in Newport Beach, California in the early 90's, we were being trained in a "non-verbal" induction technique.

The instructor used this "non-verbal" technique when working with federal investigations. This was a technique of inducing trance where there were no spoken words in the induction. There may have been a crime scene where a witness didn't speak English. The instructor would put a witness into a trance with his non-verbal technique and then he or she would be questioned by a bilingual agent about observations of the crime scene, i.e., a license plate or a description of a possible suspect.

Note: The "subconscious" stores thousands of things going on in any situation and can often be recalled under hypnosis. The "conscious mind" typically only can obtain and process up to 2 or 3% of the reality of every moment. What a neat way to extract information from someone when they can't consciously remember where they left their keys! Have you ever thought that you couldn't find your sunglasses or keys, to only then, realize they were in your hand or on your forehead!

In this non-verbal hypnosis training, we were told to pick a partner in which to practice the technique being taught. My partner tested the technique first on me. He then woke me up. Sure, I felt relaxed, but in no way hypnotized – I thought! When it was my turn to practice this non-verbal hypnosis technique, quickly my partner fell into a deep trance. Being only somewhat familiar with the power of hypnosis at that time, and yet having my partner in a deep trance, I thought to myself, "come on… this can't be real."

The astute instructor read the look on my face. His instructions to me were to emerge my partner from the trance "verbally," then for me to come onto the stage. It was as if I was being reprimanded. After doing so, in front of hundreds of students, he said, "You can't be doing what you're doing and not fully understand the power of what you're doing." My response was, "Show me. You have my full cooperation". Agreeing to accept suggestion (contract) is a part of a successful induction and is best obtained once rapport is established.

As I walked onto the stage, the instructor told me to stand straight, close my eyes and focus on an imaginary candle 12 inches in front of my forehead. After a few moments, he asked me to make my body rigid. Still hearing everything going on in the room (in the back part of my mind) and remaining focused on the candle, my body was rigid, and my mind focused. I remember intensely focusing on that candle. I knew something was going on in the room in the distance, but it didn't matter, as I kept my focus on the candle in my mind.

Then, standing straight, and rigid as instructed, yet not consciously aware of the suggestions given, I remained focused on the candle. I remember my eyes were rapidly moving (REM – Rapid Eye Movement, representative of REM sleep and a sign of hypnosis), yet I couldn't stop my eyes from moving, and still focusing on the candle in my mind, the instructor then snapped his fingers and said, "wide awake." The audience applauded wildly as it was revealed to me that during this timeless moment where I was focused on the candle, I had been lifted up by my feet and neck, six feet in the air like a solid board, with no effort on my part.

Apparently, he had given me the suggestion that my body was rigid, like a solid unbreakable and strong, solid board. When he was assured that the suggestion was fully accepted, while I was fixated on an imaginary candle, he then asked two strong men in the audience to tip me over and then lift my body above their heads. A person in the audience showed me a video of the act, as I then looked at my instructor and thanked him for demonstrating what I needed to understand. From then on, my understanding of hypnosis and the power of the mind grew further.

Note: When you are in a trance, you don't consciously know that you are in a trance! That's why it's sometimes hard to see the bad habits in ourselves, hence, "Thinking Beyond Habitual Thinking." Meditation helps us consciously see ourselves and become objective to our unconscious "thinking patterns." From there, one is better able to use self-hypnosis to influence the subconscious mind consciously, so without any effort on your part; you'll put your life on cruise control leading you to the destinations that "you" choose.

WHAT WOULD IT BE LIKE COMING OUT OF A TRANCE, OF A LIFETIME?

Have you ever had a bad dream, thinking it was real, and you awaken to feel relieved that it was just a dream?

If most people are in some level of trance within their everyday life, what would it be like if someone came out of a trance for the first time? Mostly, when I awaken participants from a trance on stage, the response is that they feel refreshed. Since there is a relaxation meditation technique which is a part of the induction process, the byproduct of the hypnosis experience is a clear mind completely free of stress. This clear mind that is experienced is an "aware, mindful" condition that is the result/goal/byproduct of meditation.

At a particular show when I emerged a woman from hypnosis, she asked, "am I still in a trance?" I immediately re-emerged her into trance, then brought her again to a "wide awake" state. When asked how she felt, she said great! She stated to me that her mind was clear, and she felt relieved and refreshed but wasn't familiar with this mind free of uncontrollable thoughts that she was used to experiencing.

I had a brief conversation with her to help her understand that she was in an "aware" state that meditation brings one to. I also mentioned that most people don't take the time to be still to experience the moment she now feels. She reflected for a moment, then broke into a sincere cry as she reflected upon her life. She then stated how her life was full of such stress and confusion with her family life, bills, and kids.

Many in our society live their whole lives in some sort of trance, good or bad. The simple process of quieting the mind and shifting one's attention to the moment will bring a person out of a trance, which is what that woman felt. This moment of awareness that impressed her mind with a level of comfort and peace is a new place that she now can seek once again within the process of meditation and understanding how to shift to mindfulness.

She asked for the Meditation CD and stated to me that she now felt she has a new tool to help her through her seemingly crazy life.

Each person has their own experience based on what state they have evolved to in their life, but the process of awakening is different for each one of us depending on their influences and perception. During a hypnosis experience, people who are familiar with meditation generally fall into a relaxed state with relative ease. Others, for the first time, experience a feeling of peace in their mind long forgotten in this stressful world we live in.

Chapter 37

"I CAN'T BE HYPNOTIZED" SO YOU THINK!

*"An entire sea of water can't sink a ship unless it gets
inside the ship. Similarly, the negativity of the world can't put
you down unless you allow it to get inside of you."*

~ Goi Nasu

*The hypnotic influence is happening all the time.
The trick is to not let it happen when it's not what you want.*

The purpose of this book is to address the many angles to understanding the full scope of the principals surrounding meditation, mindfulness, hypnosis, and power of attraction so you can begin to recognize the subtle actions of the mind we habitually deal with day to day. Once you recognize the habitual tendencies of the mind, you'll be able to have options to develop new habits to deal with life differently if you choose.

Again:

Hypnosis is a natural state of mind that happens to everyone every day.

Hypnosis is becoming subject to that which you react to.

Hypnosis is suggestion accepted.

Hypnosis occurs when suggestion breaks through the critical factor of the mind.

Note: "Emotion" tends to enhance the ability of suggestion to be accepted by the subconscious.

WE ALL ARE HYPNOTISTS HYPNOTIZING EACH OTHER ALL THE TIME

As mentioned earlier in this section, when someone or something can get you upset, then in effect, just hypnotized you. If your reaction is charged with emotion, it tends to open the door to your subconscious more easily. Your negative emotional reaction generally causes a resentment, which in effect creates the scenario of becoming hypnotized by that person or that situation. When dealing with people, you must understand you're dealing with that person's "mind trip." If that "trip" in them can get you to become upset, "that" which is inside of them is now in you.

IT TAKES TWO PEOPLE TO CAUSE AN ACCIDENT AND ONE TO STOP IT

I remember a trip I took to upstate NY state with my wife. I wanted to fly instead of drive. I'm always asked the question from people that know I am a pilot: Is flying safer or more dangerous than driving?

Other than the weather being a big factor in safety, when the weather is fine I feel flying is safer. Beyond the basic dangers, there are three decisions we make as pilots in regards to weather and safety anticipating a flight:

1. Go or don't go.

2. If you go and the weather deteriorates, do a 180-degree turn and go home.

3. If the weather declines, find an alternative airport to land and get out of the sky, rent a car or wait it out until the weather clears.

We made our decision within number 1, and we decided to "not" fly. The weather was questionable, so we drove instead.

It was a little frustrating driving as I was comparing the drive to flying instead. Two hours in the air vs. 6 to 7 hours driving each way is far more desirable. Upon the completion of our return trip, we counted over seven near fatal accidents overall that we avoided on the road. Driving is dangerous. Distracted drivers are the number one cause of automobile accidents.

INTERESTING STORY ABOUT DISTRACTED DRIVERS FROM 75 YEARS AGO

I remember my grandmother telling me about when radios first were installed in automobiles. Back in her day, cars didn't have radios as a stock item. When people started installing radios into their vehicles, there was much controversy about how they were distracting drivers and causing a possible dangerous hazard to all drivers. In May of 1935 state legislators in Connecticut introduced a bill that would have made the installation of a radio into a car subject to a $50 fine (that would be about $825 adjusted for inflation). It didn't pass.

Today, we are more distracted than ever with the cell phone and especially texting. By some government estimates, 25 percent of motor vehicle accidents in the US are a result of the driver being distracted. Currently, ten states have laws banning all drivers from using handheld cell phones and 39 states ban texting while driving.

Back to the point: When you drive, beyond being a driver you are in essence an 'accident avoider'. That's what safe drivers do. Hence, when you go through life in day to day interactions with people and daily occurrences, it's the same thing.

The message: You are always dealing with people in your daily life experiences that are unaware and subject to what is dominating inside their minds and their perceptions in that specific moment. If you are unaware of this fact, like the uncharged coil of wire picking up the energy from the charged coil, when you unconsciously react to them, what is inside them will get inside you.

The practice: Staying aware and mindful of this truth will always allow you to be in control of your associations and better allow you to communicate more effectively to all interactions in your personal and professional lives. By learning to live with mindfulness as an instant perceptual shift if necessary, you'll be better able to sense where people are coming from and disarm most situations with minimum misunderstanding.

AGAIN! THOUGHTS TO PONDER

It takes two people to create an accident and one to avoid it.

If you're not a part of the solution, you're part of the problem.

SO HOW DO YOU PROTECT YOUR MIND
FROM UNWANTED SUGGESTIONS?

Learn how to utilize the tools of the mind to master your Visionary Mind Power each when they make the most sense. In the situations outlined above, you will be able to access mindfulness in an instant when the situation finds itself useful. From there you will be better able to navigate through experience with minimal distractions from your ideal life that you create for yourself.

Chapter 38

MORE HYPNOTIC INSIGHTS MISCONCEPTIONS AND TECHNIQUES FOR SUCCESS

Understanding the process of hypnosis and getting beyond the myths will help you begin to open up to being able to use this powerful process of the mind.

SELF HYPNOSIS – *CAN I REALLY DO THIS?*

After reading up to this point, you may still be wondering if you can be hypnotized? Is it possible to actively create suggestive thoughts and images in your mind to attract desirable results? You still may fear that you could become hypnotized and lose control of yourself.

The purpose of this book is to reveal that most of us are hypnotized anyhow, and there is nothing to fear. Hypnosis is a natural process of the mind. The question is how can we re-hypnotize our minds for an amazing life beyond your present expectations.

WHAT SHOULD BEING HYPNOTIZED FEEL LIKE?

During a trance session, whether it be self-hypnosis, private hypnotherapy or stage hypnosis, you will become relaxed – but remember hypnosis is not sleep. It is a special state of mind that allows us to bypass the critical factor of the conscious mind and program the subconscious to achieve your goals and visions for new habits. These new ideas then influence your conscious mind without consideration or argument.

While one is relaxed, the mind will be fully alert and aware of the suggestions it is receiving. All outside stimuli will become irrelevant. The focus will be directly on the words of the suggestions being received as the breathing becomes light and rhythmic. There may be a distorted sense of time. It may feel like one has been in hypnosis for just a couple of minutes, even if it has been sixty to ninety minutes.

In a private hypnotherapy session, the suggestions are specific to the pre-interview revealing the goals of a session. In a self-hypnosis session, you relax the mind completely and re-affirm the affirmations you wish to have influence your subconscious for positive change. In a stage show, the suggestions are fun with the purpose to demonstrate the power of suggestion, and then at the end of my stage show, I like to leave the participants with positive motivational suggestions as well as revealing subconscious mind control techniques to their subconscious.

AN EASY SELF HYPNOSIS TECHNIQUE

A wonderful simple technique is to write down suggestions (visions of yourself that you desire as outlined in a previous chapter) in a clear-cut way on a piece of paper. When you're about to go to bed, study the suggestions. As you go to sleep, build a vision of these suggestions in your mind as if they've already happened

– feel how good that feels. As you pass from an awake state to sleep state, the doorway to your subconscious is open, and therefore a wonderful time to use self-hypnosis.

The doorway to your subconscious opens again when you're about to awaken in the morning, as you lie in bed, so relaxed when you're not ready to move, yet you know it's close to the time to wake up. This is a perfect time to remember to to use self-hyp-nosis, and re-affirm the vision of yourself again of the change you want to see for yourself. Think of one thing you can do during the day to make this vision happen and see yourself doing this. Feel the satisfaction of accomplishing your vision. Emotional feel-ing of success is the key to have your subconscious accept the suggestion.

As you rise and face the day, you won't be thinking of your self-hypnosis session so much, yet, the suggestions will be planted into your subconscious mind reminding you to stay focused on the changes you want as you go about your day. This is similar to driving home and forgetting you're driving, yet you are always moving towards your objective (home) without any effort on your part.

I'M SCARED OF HYPNOSIS THEREFORE I DON'T THINK IT WILL WORK FOR ME

It is difficult during a hypnosis session to induce a person into a trance that finds it hard to allow themselves to relax because they think that under hypnosis they will surrender all control of their behaviors to the hypnotist. This fear causes the critical factor of the mind to hold strong. However, when under hypnosis, one is in more control than when in a normal conscious state. One becomes internally focused, and the surrounding environment becomes less important and insignificant.

This fear often is present as many of us have seen zombie-like characters in the movies that are supposedly in a hypnotic state of mind, and perhaps, some have seen or heard of abuse or embarrassment of those under hypnosis by the hypnotist. From these and several other sources, common misconceptions about what hypnosis is can create resistance for those who are being hypnotized for the first time.

The truth is that for any reason, if there were an emergency or one's attention was needed, immediately one would snap out of the trance and respond appropriately. An example would be when you're driving too fast while daydreaming and don't realize it until you see the red and blue lights flashing behind you attempting to get your attention. Instantly, you emerge from the trance state and pull over.

"Emerge" means to come to an entirely awake state from a trance state. To rise and shift from your subconscious to your conscious mind. This process happens to most of us when we simply snap out of a daydream.

When hypnotized one may appear to be asleep, yet biological, the state of sleep is very different from hypnosis. The participants during a hypnosis demonstration, who are demonstrating their Visionary Mind Power, at times appear to be asleep, but simply are visualizing themselves to be limp, completely relaxed, in complete control of their state being suggested by the hypnotist. Should the suggestion be changed by the hypnotist, they would immediately be able to shift and express the new suggestion in an instant.

To command your Visionary Mind Power as you pass through your life experiences would be the ability to consciously shift your state of mind to what is most appropriate in an instant.

WHEN HYPNOTIZED, WILL I BE OUT OF CONTROL?

Many people believe that while under the trance state they will be out of control or out of touch with reality. Nothing could be further from the truth. During hypnosis your senses become heightened.

If while you're in a trance state something occurs that requires your attention, anything from the smell of smoke or the call for assistance from a loved one, the critical factor of your mind will take over and immediately emerge you from hypnosis, and you will respond appropriately.

You see, there is nothing to fear about hypnosis as it's a natural state of mind where the mind is simply relaxing. While understanding what is going on within this state of mind, you will be better able to comprehend how to use the power of self-hypnosis as a tool for behavioral change. This tool will improve your life, dramatically! All that is needed is to simply do it and allow yourself to improve at learning how to let go and accept new suggestions into your mind.

Part IV

VISIONARY MIND POWER

Integrating

MEDITATON, MINDFULNESS,

SELF-HYPNOSIS & POWER OF ATTRACTION

into your life

Chapter 39

MEDITATION & MINDFULNESS

The goal of meditation isn't to control your thoughts, it's to stop letting them control you.

Meditation helps us see the difference.

Mindfulness allows us to live the difference.

You've heard the saying, "The journey of a thousand miles begins with a single step." Start by beginning to take a period of time in the morning before you engage in your daily activities. Wake up, wash your face, brush your teeth and bring yourself to a tranquil place in the house or outside in nature. Don't think about it. Just bring yourself to a place where you can be left undisturbed and quiet and begin to feel the breath as it travels through your nose as you begin your process of meditation. Learn to be acquainted with the idea that for the next few moments, you don't need to think about anything.

Know that this is your special time, for yourself, as you begin to take a journey within your mind, for your "daily bread" of quiet contemplation, to nourish your mind mentally, spiritually and to create a solid foundation of your "ideal," to carry you through your day.

Do this for 20 days, and you'll have a new habit. As mentioned earlier, habits are created by repetition. Think of this as a wonderful investment for yourself to create a ritual that will carry you through life.

Understand what you're doing here. The rational mind will make excuses, think of distracting things to do. We need to understand that we are dealing with two forces within our mind. If all that you have read here makes sense to you, then understand the motivation to quiet your mind should not be energized with struggle or ego. As Nike says, "Just Do It."

Think of a cat. It knows the art of being still. It purrs timelessly the moment and has learned the art of being seemingly happy for no reason. It revels in the bliss of doing and thinking nothing. Calm, relaxed and very alert – mindfulness. In a split second, the attentiveness of a cat will act upon the immediacy of the moment. A moving speck of dust. A subtle sound off in the distance. The sound of a car coming into the driveway and how the sound reveals its master's car.

Be still and know the power of being conscious in the moment. Have faith that when you sit still in the moment and follow the simple exercise suggested, a new awareness will be revealed to you.

Although you may have many thoughts spinning around within, give yourself the time to quiet your restless mind. The process will awaken you to a new world that co-exists along with the world of worry, doubt, and fear. It's like a shift from one side of your mind to the other. The unsettling thoughts that cloud your perception begin to settle like the stirred up water in an ocean of waves. When the water settles on the surface and becomes calm and still, the sediments suspended in the water settle; also, one soon begins to appreciate a clearer view.

Chapter 40

SELF HYPNOSIS & POWER OF ATTRACTION

"What you think, you become.
What you feel, you attract.
What you imagine, you create."

~ Buddha

The shift in awareness revealed to you by meditation will open your mind to higher ground that will reveal the unclouded truths in your life. The wisdom revealed will be the key to seeing the answers that will offer you the natural motivation to manifest your ultimate mission for your life.

Build the vision in your imagination of the way you would like to see yourself and your life – ideal. Use your visualization power to see it as if it has already happened. See the mental picture of your ideal life every day and re-write the description as often as possible to reinforce and deepen your vision. Be sure to review the summary of your ideal and draw a mental picture in your mind before going to sleep and upon awakening in the morning. Contemplate your visions as often as you can. See them as if they have already happened. Write down any more insights that may come to you.

Create a five minute audio of your visions with your voice on your smartphone or any voice recorder that is convenient. Play this as often as possible. Remember how repetition is used by advertisers to influence your subconscious. Now it's your turn to do this for yourself.

Know that your repeated attention to your vision will activate emotion which will allow your vision to be accepted into the subconscious mind and offer you faith that this can and will manifest. Once your subconscious mind accepts the revelation, the magic of the universe will jump your mind to attention to help you notice the things that life presents to you, to act upon, as you move closer towards your purpose. These new actions might seem awkward at first, but also will feel right to you as you are fulfilling your quest and building momentum as you creatively manifest your vision.

The persistent repeating of the suggestions of your ideal will bring your mind to a place where temporary setbacks and distractions will not take you off your path. You'll understand setbacks as simple lessons on your journey to help you refine the procedure you need to learn to reach your objectives.

You're awakening your God-given ability to manifest a fantastic life.

Chapter 41

VISIONARY MIND POWER, VMP – LIVING THE MAGIC

Where did that concept come from? What does it mean to me?
What is it that I hope you will gain from understanding VPM?

VISIONARY MIND POWER

The VMP concept occurred to me one day when we were in Block Island. My wife and I often fly in the summer to Block Island from Connecticut – an island just off the coast of Rhode Island. Having a plane is most appreciated in the summer in the Northeast, as I call it the "Puddle Jumper."

Driving a car would take three to four hours each way, with traffic, waiting on lines to catch the ferry to the island, along with parking, fees and long lines. Beyond the plane to be in proper order mechanically, flying only requires good weather and takes us 25 minutes with no traffic, no rush and a relaxing, breathtaking flight with views only a high flying bird can appreciate and a $10 landing fee for the day.

We are fortunate to have the airport personal let us store our bicycles in the airport garage. We bike out to a distant remote path where cars are not allowed and pedal down these beautiful dirt roads with trees shading parts of the roadway that allows for a cool relaxed ride in the summer's heat.

Visionary Mind Power was a concept I saw in my mind while riding along that path. I stopped my bike and noted on my I-phone notes app, the principal. It seemed to me to be the concept I was looking for to describe the ability to take all the mental tools we've discussed and apply it to any and all of our experiences in life.

The art of Visionary Mind Power is nothing more than using our God given ability to manifest and create in this world we find ourselves. The tools outlined in this book will help anyone get back on track and to think beyond their habitual thinking.

Upon arriving home that day, the domain name VisionaryMindPower.com was available at which point I locked in and purchased it. From there, I started putting my thoughts together to conceive this book, writing with this new context in mind as a central theme.

Human beings are not like the animals on earth. A cat is a cat and does what cats do. A bird is a bird and does what birds do. A human is different.

We have a mind with the unique ability to choose and decide what actions we do day to day. We have a capability above all the animals. The truth is that we have free will.

Sometimes people influence us as to what they think we should do, and sometimes they pressure us about what to do. At the same time, no-one tells us what to do, and we need to figure it out ourselves. Free will is a freedom that we need to understand.

The problem is that we never had an instruction manual that

was shown to us when we were born into this world. Because of our lack of knowledge of our mind's capabilities, we risk taking this "God-given creating ability" and create undesirable circumstances. These results get conditioned into habits that lead us astray from our purpose, and many end up on paths that lead to confusion.

We may then find ourselves filled with anxiety and subtle pain. Many avoid facing and understanding the pain, and as a consequence, end up resorting to drugs or alcohol or become hardened and close the door to ever expressing their purpose and inner creativity. However, this pain can become the catalyst to seek higher ground.

We were cultured and taught by our parents, friends, teachers and the world influence that is filled with so many confusing and conflicting theories about life but often are never taught the knowledge Visionary Mind Power encompasses. It is my hope that the insights and techniques outlined in this book will help you understand the possibilities of your mind that allow you to open the doors to your God-given purpose. As you open your mind to these principals, may you awaken to the unlimited opportunities we each are offered in our day to day experiences to manifest beyond your wildest expectations of yourself.

Be bold. Dare to think and perceive differently if you choose. In doing so, you may discover new paths in your mind and life that have heart that offer you greater joy, happiness, prosperity, and purpose beyond your wildest dreams.

Ultimately the goal is to receive the gift of insight, to reveal the option to follow your heart and not your pain.

ABOUT THE AUTHOR

'The only thing in this world worth possessing is peace of mind...'

Bruce James Francisco is an author and keynote speaker, as well as a Certified Hypnotherapist and a teacher of meditation and spirituality. Born in New York, he studied at Pace University and University of Arizona, where his main studies were Marketing, Advertising, Acting and Photography. He now lives along the Connecticut shoreline in a home that he designed and built, with his wife, Kelly.

Over time, he started up several fruitful businesses, had success as a real estate developer and owner of a construction company and has had highly successful stage career as a keynote speaker and motivational stage hypnotist.

Within one of his Real Estate developments he built a very interesting home and has been featured on The Today Show, HDTV, Discovery Channel, cover NY Times Real Estate section, as well as over 40 worldwide TV networks and magazines. This unique luxury home came complete with a private airstrip and was built within the site of a former Atlas-F underground Missile base that had been underwater for over 40 years (Silohome.com).

He has written two previous books, *The Inner Experience* and *Warning Dangerous Ingredients*. With his background and unique insights from his accomplishments, he has written numerous articles for Natural Holistic and travel magazines.

His latest book, *THINKING Beyond Habitual THINKING,* is the first in the 'Awaken your Visionary Mind Power' series, and is the foundation of the message expressed within his keynote speaking for corporate events, schools, universities and other organizations.

When he has time to himself, Bruce loves keeping fit and being active outdoors. He enjoys, surfing, skiing, cross-fit, biking and trail running. He owns his own plane and loves to fly and get above the clouds into the sunshine on a dull and rainy day. Within his book he includes some powerful lessons of principal he learned as a pilot and applies them to lessons to help anyone in life.

He also devotes some of his time to helping others, running the meditations at a spiritual seeking group and providing motivational talks to kids from deprived inner-city schools, with whom he discusses issues that affect them, like bullying and drug abuse.

Bruce seems to have a mission to make a difference to the world and be an inspiration to others. His goal with his teaching is to awaken people to insights to help them exceed their expectations of themselves by understanding the tools of their mind and how to transcend habitual thinking patterns.

You can contact Bruce Francisco at:

bruce@VisionaryMindPower.com
www.VisionaryMindPower.com
www.BruceJFrancisco.com

ADDITIONAL INFORMATION

Bruce offers his appearance as a keynote speaker as well as special customized programs, training, and workshops in the United States and throughout the world geared to inspire on how the subconscious mind affects success and happiness in anyone's business and personal lives?

Why it's important for anyone to understand tools of meditation, mindfulness, self hypnosis and power of attraction?

How to overcome the hidden enemy of success that often succeeds in distracting people from keeping focused on their goals?

In this ever changing world full of distraction, it is increasingly important to have mind tools that will help keep a barbed wire fence around our minds to prevent life's distractions stealing you away from your goals and dreams.

Let Bruce develop a motivational keynote event tailored to any theme that will inspire your group to exceed expectations of themselves.

Please send your request for information or questions to the following contact address.

Visionary Mind Power
PO Box 270
Westbrook CT 06498

www.VisionaryMindPower.com
info@VisionaryMindPower.com